Spiritual Espresso
Volume III

ISBN: 978-0-578-03925-1

All Scripture quotations are from the King James Bible 1611.

Visit our website at:
oldpathsjournal.com

For more copies write to:

Allen Domelle Ministries
PO Box 5653
Longview, TX 75608
903.746.9632

Table of Contents

Provoking Others 7

Unbridled Tongues 9

Casting Your Care 11

Loving the Preeminence 13

Love While Standing 15

A Companion of Compromise 17

A Place Called Heaven 19

Open the Door 21

Let There Be No Strife 23

Ten Righteous People 25

What's God's Limit? 27

Family is a Team Not an Opponent 29

God Rewards Hard Work 31

The Wisdom of Wisdom 33

Meant for Good 35

Wastefulness Leads to Poverty 37

What Will it Take? 39

Go Forward 41

Standing Afar Off 43

Our Guardian Angel 45

Changing Who You Are 47

In the Shadow of God 49

Conflicting Responsibilities 51

Backslidden in Heart 53

Correcting Mistakes 55

Second-Hand Offerings 57

The Year of Jubile 59

Hurt by an Equal 61

Taking God's Presence for Granted 63

Nevertheless… 65

A Governed Spirit..67

What's Your Excuse This Time? 69

Wholly Followed..71

Encourage Him 73

God Delivered...75

God's Boot Camp..77

Response to Disgruntled Church Members............79

Wisdom's Silence..81

If Thou Wilt Not Hearken... 83

Nothing Between 85

A Sanctified People...87

So Did Joshua 89

Unwavering Strength for War...............................91

The LORD was with Judah 93

Again..95

Hurray for Jephthah's Daughter..........................97

Running with the Enemy 99

Ruth Clave Unto Her..101

Are You Listening?...103

Whose Side are You On? 105

God Remembers 107

Life's Unpleasantries..109

Thanks for Nothing! 111

Turning Friends Into Enemies 113

Respect the Power..115

She Came In 117

David's Friend 119

Overreacting 121

Source of Strife 123

Setting Yourself Apart From the Rest.................125

Stop Fooling Yourself.......................................127

Do Your Job 129

License to Sin 131

Dig the Ditches 133

The Power of Influence 135

Plugged Ears and Hardened Necks 137

Getting the Ear of God 139

Jabez's Prayer 141

A Strange Way to Minister 143

Responding Properly to Personal Treatment......145

David's 3 Worst Decisions 147

I Had in Mine Heart...149

Have You Made an Altar Lately?.......................151

Fortifying the Strong Holds 153

You Are a Teacher...155

Chameleon Christianity....................................157

Encouraging Your Preacher..............................159

A Successful Influence for Christ......................161

Lose Those Stripes 163

Thoughts Lead to Consequences.....................165

Building and Repairing.....................................167

Counted Faithful 169

The Power of Disloyalty 171

Facing Your Greatest Fear...............................173

Learn To Laugh 175

God Knows Your Way.......................................177

Loving Yourself 179

Opinions..181

God Can Do Every Thing..................................183

Beware of Temptation 185

Listen! 187

The Importance of Working Together.................189

Your Purpose for Sacrifice 191

Cold Love...193

What Have You Done With Jesus? 195

A Prophet Without Honor 197

Hearsay 199

A Benefit of Overcoming Temptation.............................201

Jesus, Your First Option 203

Relationships with God 205

Good Habits 208

Which Way Do You Lean? 210

Evidence for Validation 212

Position Must Be Earned 215

Thoughts About Peer Pressure....................................217

Doubting God's Miracles...220

Good Works and Almsdeeds 222

Have You Separated?..224

Repentance Brings Action 226

Provoking Others

Hebrews 10:24

"And let us consider one another to provoke unto love and to good works:"

Among the many reasons why we go to church, we find in this verse one of those reasons is that we may provoke others to love people and to do good works. What a strange reason for God to say we should go to church. Yes, we go to church for many other reasons, but one of the reasons God wants us in church is to be one who provokes others.

This word *"provoke"* means "to call into action, arouse, excite, challenge, move, and to stir up." What powerful meanings this word carries. God said when we go to church our actions at church should call others into action. We should cause others to be aroused to work for God and love others more. Our actions at church should cause others to be excited, challenged and stirred to do more good for the cause of Christ.

To be quite honest with you, in the majority of churches most people would never be provoked if they depended on the actions of other Christians to provoke them. I like to say when you go to church you are not going to church to be a spectator; you are going to church to be a participator. Your participation in the church service should, and will, cause others to participate as well. I have said many times when I preach that I would love to have a video camera to record and show people how they look during the song service and the preaching time. Most of our churches today are dead with no excitement and they would never provoke anyone to love others and do good works. Listen, when you go to churches that have an excitement during the song service and the preaching time, it provokes people when they leave to want to do more for God. If only everyone would understand the importance of trying to provoke others during the service time.

The next time you go to church, try to be one who provokes others to love and good works by your actions of being involved in the program of the church and in the church service itself. During the congregational singing, sing with enthusiasm so you can provoke others with your singing. When the preacher is preaching, participate in the preaching by saying, "Amen" loudly so as to provoke others to help make the preaching service exciting. When the invitation time comes, be the first one to walk to the altar to make a decision so that your movement may provoke others to go to the altar as well. Realize that your inaction or action will provoke others to do the same that you are doing. Choose to be the person, even if you are the only one, who provokes others unto good works by your involvement and good works during the church service.

Unbridled Tongues

James 1:26

"If any man among you seem to be religious, and bridleth not his tongue, but deceiveth his own heart, this man's religion is vain."

Years ago as a younger man, I lived out West and worked part-time on staff at a church where many of the members had horses. Because of this, it allowed me many opportunities to ride horses. Hardly a week went by without the opportunity to go horseback riding out in the plains. One of the instruments that we used to work with the horses was the bridle. To those who do not know what a bridle is, a bridle consisted of a bit that you put in the horse's mouth to control the horse. Attached to this bridle are the reins that are held in your hand. This bridle helps you control this very powerful animal that, if not controlled, it could hurt or even kill you. This bridle and bit, even though it is such a small instrument, controls this powerful animal and allows you to take that horse wherever you want to go.

God said that the tongue is like this horse; it is a very powerful member of your body. Though it is a very small part of your body, inside of the tongue is the power to destroy your whole life if it is not controlled properly. God said, of all the members of the body, you better learn to bridle your tongue. Your tongue can destroy everything for which you ever worked. In fact, in James 3:2, God said the person who is able to control the tongue is also the person who can control their body. God said in James 3:8, that the tongue is a member that cannot be tamed, it must be bridled. Our tongue gets most of us in trouble! It is when we are in a fit of rage that we say things we regret later on. It is a married couple who in a marital spat say things they wished they had never said that send hurt down deep into the heart. O how careful we must be to control our tongue.

One of the ways I have learned to control the tongue is to not say everything that I am thinking. What gets most people into trouble is they keep on talking. Let me teach you two words that most people don't like to hear, "Shut up!" I know, to some they think we don't need to say this, but sometimes we just need to shut up. It is when you talk too much that you get yourself into trouble.

Another tactic I have learned that helps me control my tongue is to wait and think before I give a response. Many times we get anxious to give a response, and we need to learn that if we will wait before we say anything we can better control our tongue. Every response we give should be a measured response. If we are not careful, our tongue will get us into trouble because without thinking we respond and later on wish we would not have said what we said.

As we think of the tongue and bridling the tongue, does your tongue control you or do you control your tongue? If you can control your tongue then you are also a person who is able to control your whole body. A person who does not control their tongue will not control their body either. Let's be careful as we go throughout this day to watch what we say and keep our tongue bridled and under control.

Casting Your Care

1 Peter 5:7

"Casting all your care upon him; for he careth for you."

I recently had a person ask me if I had anything that could help a person with severe depression. This did not shock me. As I look at our society and see all the troubles that our society has, it is no wonder that people worry themselves into depression. With the state of the economy, with the complex problems this day and age presents for people, with the pressures that our jobs place upon us and with the problems that families go through, it is no wonder that people are worried and depressed.

God commands us in this verse to cast upon Him all of our cares because He cares for us. When God used the word *"care,"* He was talking about all of our concerns, worries, anxieties and mental pain. As much as people don't like to admit that they have these problems, we all have our concerns about the future; we all have our anxieties and uneasiness about situations we face on the job and in our families; we all have our worries concerning situations that we can't seem to control. The good news is this, we have Someone Who really wants us to bring all of these cares to Him; this someone is God.

God is concerned about your cares of life. I know at times it seems that nobody is there to really care about your cares of life. It sure is comforting to know that we as Christians do have Someone Who is concerned with our cares. Now if we don't bring these cares to God, we are sure to set ourselves up for depression, misery and gloom which are the result of trying to work through these problems by ourselves. This is the difference between the Christian and the non-Christian;

11

the non-Christian only has a psychiatrist or counselor to whom they bring their problems and they can do nothing for their cares other than prescribe a medication that is a mere sedative. Christians have a God Who doesn't need to prescribe any medication, for He is the only One Who can truly help us with our cares of life.

I don't know what your worries are today, but let me assure you that you have Someone Who really wants to help you with the worries, concerns and anxieties that you face today; that someone is God. Whatever your care is today, cast that care upon God right now for He is the One Who can and will help you through this problem. You don't have to carry the weight of your care yourself; He is there to help you with this care.

Loving the Preeminence

3 John 1:9

"I wrote unto the church: but Diotrephes, who loveth to have the preeminence among them, receiveth us not."

A very interesting short story is mentioned here in this verse about a man by the name of Diotrephes. Apparently this man held some position in the church and refused to allow the Apostle Paul to have any contact with the church out of fear of losing his position, even to the extent that he would not read God's Epistle unto the people. What would cause Diotrephes to not allow even the Word of God to be read to the church? The reason was because he loved to have the preeminence in the church. He loved his position and the fact that everybody in that church would come to him. He loved being the only one who received the glory for everything being done in that church. He was so in love with his position that he felt threatened by Paul's presence. He probably felt threatened because he was afraid if Paul came, that Paul would get more attention than he would, so to protect his position he refused the Epistle to be read to the church.

This situation happens over and over again in our churches, homes, jobs and society. We have people who are so in love with receiving the glory themselves that they have become insecure about others coming in and taking away any of their glory. Some people who hold positions in a church will literally try to destroy anyone who threatens to take their position. Husbands and wives try to have the preeminence with their children and will tear down the other spouse in front of their children so that they can be the "best" parent in the eyes of their child. Employees in the workplace will not

SPIRITUAL ESPRESSO VOL 3

give credit to someone who has come up with an idea for fear they may lose their position. On and on we could go as people will sow false reports about someone or will try to destroy someone out of the fear of losing their position because of their love of having the preeminence among the people.

Loving to have the preeminence is very wrong and unhealthy for the fact simple that it creates division in the church, home and wherever it is happening. It creates insecurity in those who are leaders and insecurity in leadership is always dangerous to the cause that we are trying to accomplish. Be careful about loving to get the glory. Realize that if no one is concerned about who receives the glory and credit, more can be accomplished because everyone is working as a team. Teamwork in the home, church, workplace and in society will allow more to be done than people striving to have the preeminence among the people. Let's all work hard at being team players realizing the cause we are trying to accomplish is much greater than the position we strive to hold.

Love While Standing

Revelation 2:2

"I know thy works, and thy labour, and thy patience, and how thou canst not bear them which are evil: and thou hast tried them which say they are apostles, and are not, and hast found them liars:"

When God addressed the church at Ephesus, He addressed them as a church that stood for truth. You can look at the verse above and see this church's main works and labors were about fighting the sin and evil that was going on in their day. This church not only fought sin, but this church also fought the liberal preachers of their day who were trying to get people to compromise their stand on the old-time religion. Yet, the one thing God had against this church was that they had left their first love while fighting for truth. In the midst of their battles, apparently this church started taking these battles personally and lost the love for the people against whom they were standing. God rebuked this church for this action and commanded them to return to their *"first love."*

One of the hardest tasks that Christians will undertake in the ministry is the task of taking a stand for right and still loving those whom they take a stand against. I believe that every Christian should learn to stand for truth. We live in a day when most Christians are passive about the truth being attacked and passive about the sin that is destroying the lives around them. We need Christians who will be like the Christians in the church of Ephesus and stand for truth once again. I am constantly amazed how weak Christians are when it comes to taking a stand. Most Christians won't take that stand for truth out of fear of standing alone, but we must stand.

One thing we must be careful about, especially those who are prone to take a stand, is that we don't stop loving those whom we stand against. Just because we stand for truth does not mean we shouldn't love those whom we are fighting against. God wants His people to learn to balance the stand for truth with a love for people. Most people struggle with balancing these for you will find those who stand for truth have a hard time loving those whom they stand against; then you find those who love people abundantly have a hard time taking a stand. If we are going to be the Christians God wants us to be, we must learn to love people, and yet, stand for right and truth while we love those people.

When you stand against family members who are not living right, be careful that you don't become hateful in your stand. When standing against Christians who are living in sin or have compromised the truth, be cautious that you don't make the stand for truth a personal attack. I have always said, when fighting sin, be sure to fight the sin the person is doing but love the person who is committing the sin. Don't make the fight against sin about the person; fight the sin itself so you don't forfeit your right to help the one who is committing the sin.

Each of us must be careful that in our zealousness for truth we don't destroy the people who are doing wrong. Let's be sure to fight sin and make sin sound as ugly and wicked as we can, but let's love those who commit the sin and let them know that we still love them though they may be doing wrong. This is what God does with us and what we should do with others.

A Companion of Compromise

Psalm 15:5

"He that putteth not out his money to usury, nor taketh reward against the innocent. He that doeth these things shall never be moved."

When you study Psalm 15, you find a formula that God gives to Christians to keep them from being moved out of the tabernacle of God. In verse 1, the question is asked, *"LORD, who shall abide in thy tabernacle? who shall dwell in thy holy hill?"* This question was proposed to the LORD to find out what will keep the Christian from compromising or being moved. In this Psalm, God gives us nine answers that will keep us from compromise. I want to focus on one of those answers right now.

Debt is a companion of compromise! In the verse above you see that one of the things that will keep a person from compromise is not putting their money out to usury. In the Bible the word *"usury"* means *"interest on a debt."* In other words, God is warning us about getting into debt because debt can, and will if we are not careful, cause us to compromise.

I know we live in an age when debt seems to be the only way to survive. You must buy your house, car and even many appliances on credit. Though you must have debt, you must be careful about going into too much debt. When you decide to go into debt, never go into so much debt that if something small happens financially you will be sunk.

I have watched people over the years get themselves into such deep debt that they have to get a second job, which causes them to miss church, just to pay off the debt. Yes, debt is a part of life, but you must be wise in what debt you allow yourself to accept. Churches that go into deep debt are setting themselves up for compromise. The reason for this is because the pastor realizes he needs to keep people to pay the debt, so because of this he cuts back on his sermon which results in compromise. The Christian who goes into deep debt has a higher chance of compromise because they must find a way to pay off that debt.

My warning to you is simple; be very careful about going into debt. Remember that debt is a companion to compromise. Before you put anything on credit, be sure that what you are putting on credit is something you need and not something you want; be sure that the debt is not putting you out on a limb financially. Get counsel before you go into debt and always wait a few days before you sign papers for the debt. All of this is simply a precaution to keep you from going into unneeded debt.

Our goal is to serve God the rest of our lives. Debt can certainly keep us from doing this, so let's be careful about stepping out into the world of debt so that we will "...never be moved."

A Place Called Heaven

Revelation 21:1

"And I saw a new heaven and a new earth: for the first heaven and the first earth were passed away; and there was no more sea."

What a glorious promise we have – the promise of a place called Heaven. Yes, Heaven is a real place! It's as real as your home and the place you work. Heaven is a real place! I am so glad that God gives us this promise of a place called Heaven. I am so glad God promises that those who are saved can go to a place called Heaven. Thank God for Heaven! Let me remind you what this place called Heaven is going to be like.

It is certainly a place of splendor and majesty. It is a place that has mansions where the saints of God will live; mansions which are built specifically and uniquely by God Himself. Heaven is a place where nature will be present. We read that this place called Heaven will have a river flowing through it. Heaven will even be a place that is developed as it has streets, streets that are paved with pure gold.

Heaven is a place where the hardships of this world will be gone. In Heaven we read there will be no more tears. In Heaven we read there will be no more funerals or graveside services because death will no longer be present. In Heaven there will be no hospitals, doctor's offices or sickness for we read that in Heaven there will be no more pain. God simply puts it this way, that all the *"...former things are passed away."*

But best of all, God is in Heaven. Yes, we all look forward to being reunited with our loved ones. Spouses look forward to seeing their spouse again. Parents look forward to seeing their children again. Children look forward to seeing their parents again. Friends look forward to seeing those who have stepped on the other shore once again. But of all the things God mentions about Heaven, the best of all is we WILL see God. Christian, I know that there are many times in this life when we can become weary of what life brings our way, but let me remind you of a place called Heaven. IT IS REAL! If you are saved, you are going to go there someday.

Through this devotional, I simply wanted to remind you of this place called Heaven. Oh, I know we miss those who have gone on before, but we will see them again someday and someday soon. Oh, I know this life becomes weary, but take hope today and remember that Heaven is not that far away. So, let's get busy trying to bring as many as we can to this place called Heaven, and let's ease the pain of this world's heartaches with the thought of this real place called Heaven.

Open the Door

Genesis 4:7

"If thou doest well, shalt thou not be accepted? and if thou doest not well, sin lieth at the door. And unto thee shall be his desire, and thou shalt rule over him."

The tragic story of Cain and Abel starts with two brothers who came to offer a sacrifice unto God. We find that Abel brought of the firstlings of the flock which God accepted. The reason why God accepted this sacrifice was because it was a blood sacrifice and without the blood of a spotless lamb, the sacrifice would not have been accepted. The Bible states that Cain brought of the fruit of the ground to sacrifice unto God, but God would not accept his sacrifice. The reason being is that God will never accept man's works as a payment for his sins. The only sacrifice that is accepted by God is the sacrifice of the lamb. After God had rejected the sacrifice of Cain, He came again to Cain in the verse above and told him that if he would do right and sacrifice a lamb that God would accept him again. In fact, God so desperately wanted Cain to do right that He even had the sacrifice sitting at the door. All Cain had to do was open the door and his deliverance from sin was right there.

As I think of this story, I think of two principles we can learn. First of all, God so desperately wants everyone to get saved so He has provided the plan and made it possible for everyone to get saved. All that we have to do is open the door of our heart and accept Christ as our Saviour and we can go to Heaven. Salvation is not difficult. Jesus did all the difficult work for us. He was the sacrificial Lamb Who died for our sins. God, desiring to make salvation as easy as He could for us, said that all we had to do was call on Him and He would save us. Nothing else has to be done for salvation other than to call on God and accept the payment that Jesus paid on the cross and you can be saved.

The second principle I believe we can learn is that God also desperately wants us to do right. So much so that He will provide a way out of every temptation if we will only open the door to His ways and follow them. Everyone has a choice when faced with the temptation of sin. We can open the door and run from the sin, or we can keep that door closed, commit the sin and pay the horrible penalty for that sin. There is no temptation that you cannot overcome for God will provide a way out of that temptation if only we will open the door and flee.

Whatever sin you face today, remember God has provided a way to deliver you from that sin. Open the door to God and ask for His help to overcome that sin. It is that simple. We simply have to accept it. Whatever you do, don't rebel and keep the door closed for that will only lead to heartache. Open the door and accept God's help to overcome sin, and you will find that God will help you overcome sin if you will only open the door.

Let There Be No Strife

Genesis 13:8

"And Abram said unto Lot, Let there be no strife, I pray thee, between me and thee, and between my herdmen and thy herdmen; for we be brethren."

I find in this verse a statement that seems to be the cry of people today and that statement is, *"...Let there be no strife, I pray thee, between me and thee...for we be brethren."* In the political realm you constantly hear the politicians crying for everyone to get along. Just recently I heard of a squabble going on in a political party over its leader and a radio commentator. Among Fundamentalists, I constantly hear people asking why everyone can't get along. Again, recently I had a conversation with a preacher who was irate that Baptists were fighting each other. He questioned why everyone was fighting and could not get along so the "greater" purpose could be accomplished.

My answer to all of these is found in this verse. The reason why there was strife between Abram's herdsmen and Lot's herdsmen was that truth was at stake. When you read the following verses you see that Lot and his herdsmen were trying to bring in compromise and Abram was standing for that which he always stood: truth.

When truth is attacked there will always be strife and peace cannot be obtained because there are those of us who believe that standing for truth is very important. Though no one, and I emphasize **no one**, likes the battles and the fighting that goes on among our ranks, when truth is at stake people must stand up and fight for truth. When a stand is being taken for truth, there will always be strife.

As we look further into this story, we find that it was Lot who was causing everyone not to get along. It was his stance of compromise that was causing the herdsmen to be at strife. Abram was the one who told Lot they could get along if he would just live right, but it was Lot's fault that the strife and contention existed because he wanted compromise and not truth. Is it not interesting that the one who tries to bring in compromise is the one calling for peace? Those who want us to compromise what we believe are always the ones who want everyone to get along. It is usually the compromisers who are the ones who complain that everyone needs to get along. This is not always the case, but the majority of the time this is true.

So, you wonder why we have strife in our nation's political parties, our churches, among Fundamentalists and even in our homes? The answer is because when truth is attacked those who love truth will stand up and fight for truth and, because of the compromisers actions, strife will exist. Let's be careful not to love peace so much that we let truth die. If strife must exist for the sake of truth being held up, then let's have strife. If we must choose between having peace through compromise or having truth through strife, ALWAYS choose truth. Yes, we don't like strife, but strife will exist whenever truth is attacked.

Ten Righteous People

Genesis 18:23

"And Abraham drew near, and said, Wilt thou also destroy the righteous with the wicked?"

Certainly one of the most well-known stories in the Bible is the story about the destruction of Sodom and Gomorrah. As you read this story, you learn that Abraham and God had a conversation about how many people needed to be in the city in order for God not to destroy these cities. Abraham, bargaining with God, asked God if He would destroy Sodom if there be found fifty righteous people in the city. Abraham continued his bargaining all the way down to ten righteous people. God said if He could find ten righteous people in this city then He would not destroy it.

In this story there are many lessons we could discuss, but I want to focus on one lesson. Abraham asked God if He would destroy the city if ten righteous people could be found in the city. God told Abraham if ten righteous people could be found, He would not destroy the city. Imagine if this was your city that God was talking about. Put your city's name in this story and ask yourself this question, "If God were looking for ten righteous people in my city, would I be the contributor to the number of ten?" What a sobering thought this is as many times we never make the stories in the Bible personal. Too many times we look at these stories and think that God would never do this to our city, nation or to us personally. Though God may not send fire and brimstone down to destroy your city, He can still destroy it in whatever fashion He chooses.

Now let's bring this story even closer to home as we think about the ten righteous people being found. Let's just say that you are one of the ten, this means now we need nine righteous people for God not to destroy your city in the scenario that I have presented. If God were to go through your city looking for the ten righteous people so He would not destroy your city, could He find nine other righteous people that you have influenced to live a righteous life? Yes, every one of us ought to live a righteous life, but each of us ought to also try and influence others to live righteous. For instance, are you influencing people in your church to live right or are you causing problems in your church by going around and tearing down those in authority? Instead of causing problems in our churches, we should be trying to influence people to live righteous lives. In your neighborhood, whom have you influenced lately to live a righteous life? In your work place, whom have you influenced to live a righteous life? Are you the righteous influence in your home? You see, we ought to live a righteous life, but we should also try to influence others to live righteous. We should be the righteous influence in our homes, churches, neighborhoods, work places and nations.

If God were to try and find ten righteous people in your city, would you be one of the righteous and would you be one of the righteous who has influenced nine others to be righteous? Let's work at being an influence of righteousness to everyone with whom we come in contact.

What's God's Limit?

Genesis 22:1

"And it came to pass after these things, that God did tempt Abraham, and said unto him, Abraham: and he said, Behold, here I am."

A very interesting statement is made in this verse as the Bible says *"...that God did tempt Abraham..."* When we see the word *"tempt"* we immediately think of being lured to do something wrong, but we can always be assured that God would NEVER tempt us to do wrong. Yet, it seems as though God was tempting Abraham to do something wrong because He asked Abraham to take his only son, Isaac, and offer him as a burnt offering to the LORD. Though Abraham did not understand this request, we see that Abraham did not question God and immediately obeyed God. We find later in this chapter in verses 16-17, that Abraham's response and willingness to give his only son back to God resulted in God's blessings. Abraham didn't limit what God could have, and thus God did not place any limits on the blessings which He bestowed on Abraham.

What is the limit that you have put on what God can have in your life? Abraham proved there was no limit and God proved there was no limit to His blessing. Too many times we put a limit on what God can have in our lives and this limit is also the limit to which God will bless us. When we read this story, we must make this story personal and ask ourselves what we would have done if we were Abraham.

Think about this, what limit have you placed on God in your life? What is it that God cannot have? If God asked you for your last dollar, would you give it? If God asked you to lose everything you have for His cause, would you be willing?

If God asked you to give your child to serve Him away from your homeland, would you allow it? What is it in your life that God cannot have?

When God asked Abraham for his only son, Abraham proved to God that there was nothing in his life that God could not have. We need to realize that to the degree we limit God is the same degree to which we limit God's blessings on our lives. We are ultimately the one who determines the degree of God's blessing on our lives. So, to whatever degree you want God to bless you in your life is the same degree you must be willing to give to God.

Just ask yourself this question, what is the limit you have placed on God? When you answer this question, you also answer how much of God's blessings you will have on your life.

Family is a Team Not an Opponent

Genesis 30:1

"And when Rachel saw that she bare Jacob no children, Rachel envied her sister; and said unto Jacob, Give me children, or else I die."

The life of Jacob was not only a life of deception, but we also see that it was a life of competition between family members. When you study Jacob's life you see the competing between family members started with his mom and dad. Then this spirit of competition carried on between him and his brother Esau. Now we see his wives Rachel and Leah competing with each other to see who could be the favorite wife. Later on in this chapter, Jacob competed with his father-in-law about who had the most. On and on it goes that Jacob's life was filled with deception mostly because of the family competing with each other. The results of all this competing between family members was heartache all throughout Jacob's life.

Nothing good comes from family members competing with each other about who is the best or who is the closest. Home is not supposed to be a place of competition. Home is supposed to be a place where family members work together to produce a good home and serve God.

Mom and dad, stop trying to compete with each other about who is the best parent. Why would parents try to turn their children against the other parent realizing they are married to that person? You will never turn out good children when your children see parents' attacking each other behind each other's back trying to be the number one parent. Your goal as parents should be to turn out children who love both parents and serve God. As long as parent's compete, this will not happen.

Likewise, brothers and sisters should not be allowed to compete. What I mean by this is every child should be treated the same, and no child should be the favorite child. When you let your children fight and squabble with each other to be the favorite child, this will cause them to fight with each other for the rest of their lives. Nothing good comes from family members competing to be better than each other.

Let's be careful not to make our home a battlefield of spouses and siblings competing to see who is the best, instead let's make our families a team that works together realizing the end result will be a close family that will accomplish more for God just as God intended.

God Rewards Hard Work

Genesis 31:6

"And ye know that with all my power I have served your father."

One of the greatest qualities lacking in our society is people who are willing to work hard. When you go to the average workplace, you see people who slack off in their work and never give all their power and energy to their work. In the average household you have parents who do not work hard in the house, and this results in turning out children who have no work ethic. This is a problem that effects the production in the workplace, the quality of the products produced and the price of goods in society.

Jacob made a statement to his wives as he readied himself to leave his father-in-law. Jacob said, *"...with all my power I have served your father."* He was saying that he worked hard, and though Laban had not rewarded him for his hard work, God saw how hard he had worked and rewarded him accordingly by blessing him with many cattle according to the agreement he and his father-in-law had made.

God rewards hard work! I know that in many workplaces it seems that hard work cannot be rewarded because people are promoted by their seniority and not by the amount of work they produce. Though this may seem to be the case, we need to always understand that God sees how hard we work, and God can and will reward us for our hard work. Hard-working people will always find a way to work because working hard is a part of their character. Of all the areas in which we need a revival; one is in the area of working hard. Every Christian should be the hardest working person in their workplace. Though the world may not like our positions or what we believe, they should always want to hire a Christian because a Christian works hard and is dependable.

Parents, if you instill any character trait in your children, be sure to instill in them the trait of working hard. Don't let your children get by with doing a half-way job in the house. When you give them a job, make them work hard for you are training them to excel in the future. It may seem that you are being cruel at the time, but in the long run you are helping them, and they will realize it when they get older. To the adult who reads this, always find yourself working hard wherever you work. Never be the person who stands around; always be the person who works harder than everyone else and produces more than everyone else.

Though you may think you are not getting rewarded for your hard work, God sees how hard you work and He will reward you for doing what is right.

The Wisdom of Wisdom

Proverbs 8:35-36

"For whoso findeth me findeth life, and shall obtain favour of the LORD. But he that sinneth against me wrongeth his own soul: all they that hate me love death."

If I could tell you that I know someone who could show you the mistakes that others made and how they made them, wouldn't you want to know that person? If I could tell you I know someone who has watched every successful person become a success and helped them to become a success and would like to do the same for you, I would imagine you would be very anxious to meet this person. If I told you I know someone who was around before the world was ever created and had a part in making the world, and this person is the same person who we talked about above, then most certainly this person is someone worth getting to know. According to this chapter in Proverbs, wisdom is that person you need to get to know.

In this chapter God personifies wisdom and says in the beginning of the chapter that wisdom cries out for people to use Him. He shows us that wisdom was the way of the LORD before there was ever an Earth created, and wisdom was the One Who was by the LORD when He created this Earth in which we live. All in all, God was trying to get us to see the importance of getting wisdom.

You would think that every person alive would try to get the wisdom from wisdom so they would know how to live. In fact, God says those who find wisdom and use wisdom find life and will obtain favour of the LORD. Whatever you do in your life, one thing that should become your closest companion is wisdom.

Where do we find this wisdom? Where do we get this wisdom? God tells us in James 1:5 that if you want wisdom then ask God for wisdom, for God is the giver of wisdom. You see, in the pages of the Word of God is wisdom for every day living. There is wisdom in getting wisdom, for in wisdom you will find the answer for what you are going to face today and the rest of your life. Whatever you do, don't offend wisdom by not using him, for those who forsake wisdom will see death in whatever they pursue.

In everything you do, be sure to ask God for wisdom. Before you drive your car, ask God to give you wisdom in driving the car and which path to take. Before you cook a meal, ask God to give you wisdom in cooking that meal. Before you open a book to study at school, be sure to ask God to give you wisdom to study and learn. Before you do anything, always whisper a prayer to God asking Him for wisdom to do that task.

Remember, the wisdom of having wisdom is that wisdom that is followed will give life and favour with God. Never start any task without first getting the wisdom to do that task; that wisdom comes from God. Always remember that wisdom has never made a mistake and will never make a mistake. Pursue the wisdom of God which has made all who use it successful and will also make you successful if you follow its advice.

Meant for Good

Genesis 50:20

"But as for you, ye thought evil against me; but God meant it unto good, to bring to pass, as it is this day, to save much people alive."

Joseph learned a very valuable lesson concerning the affliction that he had gone through, which helped him to not become bitter against those who caused the affliction. That which he learned was that God sent the affliction his way so that he could be a help to many others. Yes, his brethren intended evil for Joseph, but God took the evil works of Joseph's brethren and turned them into good for the sake of many people. Joseph learned that he was the tool of God to help others. He learned that in order to be that tool he must go through affliction, but that affliction which he would go through was sent to him to accomplish God's plan of helping others.

Of all the purposes and reasons why people go through trials in their lives, this lesson that Joseph learned needs to be learned by us in order to keep our trials from making us bitter. We must realize that trials, as hard and bitter as they may be, are sent our way so that we can be a help to others. Until you realize this, every hard time that you go through will make you a bitter person.

I don't know what you are going through today as you read this, but are you allowing the hard times which you are going through to be a tool to help others, or are you griping and complaining and becoming bitter at God for sending the hard times your way? Whether or not you realize it, God is trying to allow you to be a help to save many people from their heartache. Every trial sent our way is there for the help of others. Instead of letting the trial become evil in your eyes, let the trial you are facing today become good by using it to help others.

Your trial will become evil or good depending upon how you use it. If you look at the trials that you face as a hardship and dwell on them, then that trial will become evil to you and will cause you to get bitter. If you take the trial you are facing and use it to help others who are going through the same thing, then that trial will become a good thing to you. So you have the power to make your trials good or bad all depending upon how you use them.

I implore you today to take your trial and use it to help others who face the same heartache. By doing this, your trial will not only help save many others, but your trial will also become good in your eyes. Let's work at taking our heartaches and trials and using them as a tool to help others.

Wastefulness Leads to Poverty

Proverbs 10:4

"He becometh poor that dealeth with a slack hand: but the hand of the diligent maketh rich."

When I was in Bible College, I had some relatives who lived in the area and I frequently went over to their house and spent time with them. Because they had no children, they took care of me as if I was their own, which I always enjoyed. Many times they would take me out to eat to give me a break from the dining hall food. When the meal was over, I would watch them gather all the leftovers and ketchup packets to take home so that nothing was wasted. This always amazed me, but I learned that the reason they did this was because they had gone through the Great Depression and learned during that time not to waste anything.

God teaches us this same lesson in this verse. He said, *"He becometh poor that dealeth with a slack hand..."* The word *"slack"* means "careless, idle, lazy, negligent and sloppy." God was saying the person who is careless with what they have and lazy, negligent and sloppy in how they handle their possessions and money will one day be a poor person. God was teaching us to take care of everything we have and not to be a wasteful people.

I really believe that one of the reasons our nation is in the mess she is in is because our society has become a very wasteful society. We should recognize that everything we have is given to us by God. Because it is given to us by God, we should not be wasteful in dealing with our possessions, money or food.

Be careful about being wasteful with your food. When you go to a restaurant, instead of wasting food, buy one order and share it with the children who will not eat their whole plate. At home when a meal is cooked, be careful not to be wasteful with the food God has provided for you. Don't be a person who makes too much or puts too much on your plate and then throws the food away. This is wasteful, and this is not how God would want us to deal with the food He has given to us.

Don't be sloppy and negligent in the care of your possessions. You may not have the newest things, but take care of the things you have. God has provided your needs as He promised He would, now don't you be slack in caring for that which God has provided.

When it comes to money, be careful that you are not careless in the spending of your money. Always spend every penny carefully. Those who are careless in how they spend their money will one day have no money. Look at your receipts and make sure that you are not being overcharged. Look at your bills and be sure the company who has billed you is not charging you for something you did not want or purchase. This is being diligent with your money.

God's people should not be a wasteful people. We should be diligent with what God has given to us. When God sees our diligence in the care of what we have, then He will be more apt to give us more for He knows we will take care of what we are given. Remember a slack and wasteful hand leads to poverty; a diligent hand leads to riches. Be diligent with everything you have!

What Will it Take?

Exodus 12:31

"And he called for Moses and Aaron by night, and said, Rise up, and get you forth from among my people, both ye and the children of Israel; and go, serve the LORD, as ye have said."

This story of Pharaoh and the ten plagues is a very sad story. It finally took the death of his firstborn to get him to do what God had commanded him to do. Think about this, nine other plagues had literally ravished and destroyed the land of Egypt according to Exodus 10:7, and yet he would not obey God and let the people go to worship God. Finally, God had to take his firstborn son, the son whom no doubt was the heir of his kingdom, to get him to obey.

How sad this story is, but how common this story becomes in the lives of Christians today. I am constantly amazed how people will continue to go on in their sin even though their life has been destroyed by sin. Because God could not get a Christian's attention any other way, He had to take a loved one from them to get them to do what He made them to do. You see, sin will affect many innocent people. Unfortunately, many innocent people have to suffer because of the sin of someone else. You would think that people would get right with God, but sad to say they often do not.

I wonder as I write this devotional, to the one who has refused to let go of some pet sin, what will it take for God to get you to do what He has asked you to do? To the one whom God called to serve Him full-time in the ministry, what will it take for you to follow His calling? To the one who is living in sin, what is God going to have to do to get you to get right? To the rebellious Christian, to what degree will God have to punish you to get you to come back to Him? Is God going to have to go to the point that He takes a loved one for you to get right? Are you going to force God's hand and make God have to punish you to this degree? Yes, I have seen many times that it took the death of a loved one to get someone to come back to God. Don't let this be you!

Each of us need to look at our lives and find the sin that we have held onto for so long and get right before God must take extreme measures to get our attention. Don't be so hard-headed that God must take a loved one to get you to obey His commands. Be a Christian who has a tender heart. Be one who gets right at the first poke of conviction upon your heart. Be a Christian who has a tender heart, ever willing to do what God wants you to do so that you never experience the punishing hand of God.

Go Forward

Exodus 14:15

"And the LORD said unto Moses, Wherefore criest thou unto me? speak unto the children of Israel, that they go forward:"

As you read this verse you will see that the very first command God gave to the children of Israel after leaving the land of Egypt was to go forward. In this chapter, the children of Israel had just seen the mighty hand of God work for them by sending the plagues upon Pharaoh and his people. The last plague, the plague of the Passover, was the applying of the blood on the doorposts of the house. All who had applied the blood would not lose their firstborn to death. Now they are out of the land, and they faced the Red Sea as the great border. What a great obstacle that they faced. Surely to them it seemed an impossible obstacle to cross. But God told Moses to tell the people that they were to go forward, and when they would go forward they would see the mighty hand of God work for them once again.

Every day Christians face many obstacles in their lives. To many, these obstacles seem to be obstacles that cannot be overcome. Instead of standing there complaining about the obstacle, what every Christian needs to do is go forward by faith and trust God that He will help you through the obstacles.

When it comes to the will of God, we always need to remember that God's will is forward. God NEVER tells us to retreat, and God's will is always forward. When you move backwards or lateral in your Christian life, you are not doing what God would have you to do. God would have you to move forward.

I know that sometimes the Christian life can get hard, but you must move forward even though it may seem impossible to move forward. You will never help yourself by going backwards; you will always help yourself by going forward. The next time you are tempted to go back to an old place, an old relationship or something in the past, remember, God's will is not backwards but God's will is forward.

Today as you go throughout your daily tasks, make every decision based upon the fact that God's will is forward. You will never regret going forward for that is the direction that God wants you to move. It may be scary at times, and it may even seem impossible, but remember, it's when you move forward that God's mighty hand will be evident in your life.

Standing Afar Off

Exodus 20:18

"And all the people saw the thunderings, and the lightnings, and the noise of the trumpet, and the mountain smoking: and when the people saw it, they removed, and stood afar off."

They say the average amount of time that a person serves God is seven years. That means in seven years of the average Christian's life, they serve God and then waste the remainder of their years pretty much doing nothing. How sad that the majority of a person's life is wasted being distant from God.

The children of Israel show us one of the steps downward that take us away from God. Notice in this verse that when talking about the children of Israel God said, *"...they removed, and stood afar off."* When the people started distancing themselves from the presence of God, they were setting themselves up to leave God later on in their lives.

This happens quite often among Christians who end up quitting on God. I have watched Christians who were on fire for God remove themselves from that which gave them fire and enthusiasm only to be distant from God's presence. You must be very careful that you don't become like the Israelites in standing afar off from God.

When it comes to God's work in the church, don't stand afar off but get up close by getting involved in the church. Be careful that you don't become a church member who only attends and never gets involved with anything. If all you do is attend church and never involve yourself with your church, you will find yourself standing afar off from God's presence which only leads to coldness of heart.

When it comes to walking with God in your private time, don't stand afar off, but daily have a personal time with God in prayer and Bible reading. Those who never have a personal time with God will find themselves being distant from God. You cannot rely on the food that God has given to others; you must get your own spiritual food daily from God's Word. You must have your own time with God in prayer and not be distant from God by letting others do all the praying.

Have you removed yourself from God and do you stand afar off from His presence? Do you find yourself having a cold and indifferent heart? The best way to overcome this distant relationship with God is to involve yourself in His work which is through the church. Get involved in a soul-winning ministry to see others saved. Be sure that you don't become like those who drop all their responsibilities and stand afar off. Sit up front in the church services where the fervor of the preaching and singing is better felt and noticed. It is not always comfortable being close to the presence of God, but in His presence you will find the greatest blessings.

Our Guardian Angel

Exodus 23:20

"Behold, I send an Angel before thee, to keep thee in the way, and to bring thee into the place which I have prepared."

Years ago I heard a story of a missionary who was on the field in an area where cannibals were present. This missionary was in his house when the cannibals came to kill the missionary and his family. As they arrived at the house, the missionary knowing what they came for, fell on his knees with his family and started praying asking God to protect them from these cannibals. As I remember the story, the cannibals left after a few minutes to the surprise of the missionaries. Later on the missionary led the tribe leader to Christ and then asked him why they left that day. The tribe leader said that there was a host of armed men around the missionary and his family who these cannibals could not get through. What an amazing story! I believe that this band of armed men who the missionary could not see was the guardian angel that God had sent to protect him and his family.

According to this verse, God has sent an angel before us to *"...keep thee in the way..."* The word *"keep"* means "to guard." God gives each one of us an angel to protect us as we serve Him. What a comforting thought that we have a guardian angel about us all the time!

I must also show you that God warns us in the next few verses to beware of this angel, to obey his voice, and to not provoke him. God warns us explicitly that by obeying him we will procure protection, but by disobeying this angel we provoke him opening ourselves up for punishment. When we obey this angel, he will protect us in the way we walk and will guide us as we go through life. Yes, though the angel guides us, we will still have hard times. Wars will still come, but he is there to protect us as we serve God.

I know many times we joke about our guardian angel working overtime to protect us as we do some dumb things, but it is not a joke. God has given us an angel to protect us. Because of this we should take comfort in knowing that wherever we are at this moment God's angel is there to protect us and guide us. Listen to him as God has given him orders to guide you in the way. Let's be careful in our daily lives that we listen, and not provoke the angel God has sent to protect and guide us.

Changing Who You Are

Exodus 34:29

"And it came to pass, when Moses came down from mount Sinai with the two tables of testimony in Moses' hand, when he came down from the mount, that Moses wist not that the skin of his face shone while he talked with him."

One of the most refreshing things you can see in life is a couple who have been happily married for quite a long time. When you talk to them, they both seem to know what the other is thinking or is about to say because they have been with each other for so long. What is even more interesting is when they have been married for quite a long time they seem to belong to each other because they almost look like each other. Their countenances have changed because they have spent so much time with each other.

In this chapter we read how Moses went back to God to receive the Commandments and spent forty days and nights with God. The Bible states that when Moses came down from Mount Sinai that the skin of his face shone. This glow that Moses had was nothing more than the reflection of God upon him because he had been with God for so long. His time with God literally changed his countenance just like anyone who spends time with God today will change more into the likeness of God.

Many times people say they have a hard time changing. Yet, in all reality the only reason they are not changing is because they are not spending enough time with God. If a person would spend time with God, they would change more into the image of God. You cannot spend time with God without looking like you have been with Him. The only reason we don't look more like God and instead look more like the world is because we spend more time with the world than we do with God.

If you have something in your life that you need to change, I have the answer for you; spend more time with God and you will see yourself change into what God wants you to be. The reason you don't look more like you ought to is because you are not spending enough time with God. The answer to overcoming sin is spending time with God. The answer to changing your attitude is spending time with God. The answer to overcoming a vice in your life is spending time with God. You may not see the change in yourself immediately, but if you spend enough time with God you WILL change.

You may say you don't have enough time to spend more time with God, but may I say if you want to change badly enough you will find time to spend with God. Spending time with God WILL change you and the way you are perceived among men, for you cannot spend time with God without changing. When you spend time with God, you will not change Him into what you are but He will change you into what He is. Whatever you do, find the time to spend with God so He can change you into His image and likeness.

In the Shadow of God

Exodus 37:1

"And Bezaleel made the ark of shittim wood: two cubits and a half was the length of it, and a cubit and a half the breadth of it, and a cubit and a half the height of it:"

It is interesting to me that when God chose a man to build the Ark of the Covenant He chose Bezaleel as that man. The Ark of the Covenant was not only the place which the mercy seat rested, but it was also the piece of furniture in the temple that represented the presence and power of God. The Ark of the Covenant was so sacred that God even designated a special way of carrying it. The priests were the only ones who were to carry this piece of furniture, but also the priests were the only ones to go into the Holy of Holies once a year. This room was where the Ark of the Covenant rested when the children of Israel were not journeying. The reason I think its interesting that God chose Bezaleel to be the one who built the ark is because of the meaning of his name. The name *"Bezaleel"* means *"in the shadow of God."*

I believe God wanted us to understand that only by walking in the shadow of God will a man ever experience the power of God upon his life. Do you realize the significance of walking in the shadow of God? Not only does walking in the shadow of God mean that you will obtain the power of God upon your life, but it also means that by walking in His shadow there is protection. I promise you Christian, when you are in God's shadow you have nothing to fear.

In order to be in someone's shadow you must be near them. You will never be in God's shadow by walking in the world. You will only succeed in being in the shadow of God by serving Him. When you serve Him in His shadow, you will have the power and protection of God upon your life.

I ask you, are you close enough to God to be in His shadow? Whose shadow are you walking in today? You are walking in someone's shadow. Is that shadow the shadow of the world? Is the shadow that you are walking in the shadow of materialism and worldliness?

It is no wonder that God chose Bezaleel to be the one who should build the Ark of the Covenant, for when a man walks in the shadow of God he no doubt will have God's power and protection on his life. Always remember, the only way you will ever walk in God's shadow is to spend time in prayer. Psalm 91:1 says that those who dwell in the secret place of God, which is prayer, will abide under His shadow. Be sure to walk in God's shadow today by spending time with Him in prayer and you will have His protection and power upon your life for this day.

Conflicting Responsibilities

Leviticus 10:7

"And ye shall not go out from the door of the tabernacle of the congregation, lest ye die: for the anointing oil of the LORD is upon you. And they did according to the word of Moses."

The truth that I want to present in this devotional comes from a very sad story of two young men who disobeyed God by offering strange fire unto the LORD. Because of their actions, God sent fire down from Heaven and killed these two young men. These young men were the sons of Aaron who was also the high priest. God told Moses to tell Aaron that he was not to go and weep for his sons and leave his responsibility of being the high priest to go to their funeral. God said he and his sons were to continue their responsibilities that He had commanded them to do, and let his brethren take care of the young men who had died.

Sometimes in life responsibilities seems to conflict. When responsibilities conflict, many people find it hard to choose which responsibility they are to do. You must always remember that when responsibilities conflict always choose the responsibility that God placed as the higher responsibility.

By way of illustrations let me explain what I am talking about. When the responsibilities of church and work conflict, always choose church over work. God said to seek Him first and then He would take care of the rest for us. Too many times I see individuals choose their job over church, and this will only result in God pulling His blessings from us. Serving God and going to church is a more important responsibility according to the Bible.

When the responsibility of doing God's will conflicts with family, you choose God's will first. When my mother and I talked the last time before her home going, she told me that when she went to Heaven I was not to cancel a meeting to take care of her funeral arrangements. When she went home to be with the LORD, I was preaching a meeting in Pennsylvania and I kept my promise to my mom and my responsibility to my God to do His will first. God always honors us when we put Him first.

Over and over again in life it will seem that responsibilities conflict, when they do we must be sure to choose the right responsibility. When they conflict, always choose the responsibility that God considers a higher responsibility first. By doing this you not only show God that you consider Him the highest responsibility in your life, but you will also be blessed by God for making this choice. Be careful what you choose when your responsibilities seem to conflict.

Backslidden in Heart

Proverbs 14:14

"The backslider in heart shall be filled with his own ways: and a good man shall be satisfied from himself."

Is it possible for a person to be doing the works that God has commanded them to do and yet not be right with Him? The answer to this question is a definite "yes." In this verse God talks about a person who is backslidden in their heart. Notice, God did not say their actions showed they were backslidden, but the motives of the actions is what showed they were backslidden.

God said the person who is backslidden in their heart is the person who is filled with his own ways. Everything about the person who is backslidden in their heart has to be about them. God even gives the comparison in this verse by saying the good man is satisfied *"...from himself."* The good man gets his satisfaction in life from the outside by helping others, while the backslider in heart gets their satisfaction from making everything revolve around them.

I would assume that by you reading this devotional you are most likely trying to serve God. Most people who are not serving God are not going to take time out of their day to read a devotional. The one thing I must caution you about is letting your heart be backslidden. If you have a backslidden heart, you will one day be backslidden in action. Whatever your heart does right now will eventually be what you become on the outside. This is why we must take care of a backslidden heart.

Are you backslidden in your heart? Does everything in life have to revolve around you? Is serving God all about you?

Are you the type of person who when serving God you must get the credit or you will not do it at all? This is a person who is backslidden in heart. In your home life, does everything have to revolve around you? Do you make your marriage miserable because if it is not what you want you make it known to your spouse? This is the action of a person who is backslidden in heart. In the home, do your parents have to do everything to please you or else you become a terror in the home? This is nothing more than being backslidden in heart. Even on the job, when you make everything revolve around you, you are acting like a person who is backslidden in heart.

Be careful about being backslidden in heart. Check your actions of the past week and see if those actions required that everyone do what you wanted them to do. If they did not do what you wanted, did you show your displeasure? There are many people who are good people and still do what they are supposed to do, but while doing these tasks they are backslidden in their heart. Let's strive to not be a backslider in action or in heart. Let's make sure that our actions and our heart are right with our God.

Correcting Mistakes

Leviticus 16:1

"And the LORD spake unto Moses after the death of the two sons of Aaron, when they offered before the LORD, and died;"

If we're honest with ourselves, everybody makes mistakes in life. There is not a person alive who hasn't done something wrong and then looked back and wished they could have done something different to avoid that problem. The secret to never repeating what caused the mistake is to figure out what caused it and correct it so it never happens again.

In the verse above, God came to Moses *"...after the death of the two sons of Aaron..."* Now let me make this clear before we go any further, God NEVER makes a mistake! The biggest reason why the story of Nadab and Abihu happened is because they did not listen to God. Because God is a loving God as well as a just God, He goes back to Moses to set up a plan to avoid the same problem in the future. God was making sure that this wouldn't happen again because He is never pleased with having to punish His children.

In our lives, we must learn from our mistakes and from the mistakes of others. Never let problems which have arisen and mistakes which have been made continue to go on. The best way to make sure these things never happen is to correct the problem after it has happened. Let me quickly give you some thoughts on how to avoid making the same mistakes again.

First of all, be sure to get right with God over the mistake you've made. When you do something wrong or have made a mistake in life, be sure that you get any wrong you have done right with God. Always get everything right in your life with God when you have done something wrong.

Secondly, immediately following the mistake, find out what caused the mistake. When mistakes have been made, you should study them to figure out the cause. The best time to learn from your mistake is when it is fresh on your mind. How foolish it would be not to learn from our mistakes the first time. Sometimes the best teacher in life is on-the-job training.

Thirdly, set up a plan to avoid the same mistake. If you studied what caused the problem, you should know how to avoid that problem. Your study of what caused the problem is not enough, you must set up a plan that will keep you from doing the same thing over again. If you don't set up a plan to avoid that problem again, you'll make the same mistake again.

Next, you must be sure to follow the plan you set up. Having a plan without following that plan is like having no plan at all. It would be like having rules in a school and then not following the rules you set up. We MUST be sure to follow the plan and rules we have set up that help us to avoid having the same problem again.

Last of all; daily ask God to help you avoid doing the same thing that caused you to mess up in the first place. Ask God to keep you from that which caused you to make a mistake. God is the only One Who can help you avoid mistakes. Without His help, we will fail. Take these steps and implement them the next time you make a mistake, and see if you can't avoid making the same mistake again. Whether it's at your workplace, school, church, home or elsewhere in your life, you will make mistakes, but you must follow these steps to avoid making those same mistakes again.

Second-Hand Offerings

Leviticus 22:24

"Ye shall not offer unto the LORD that which is bruised, or crushed, or broken, or cut; neither shall ye make any offering thereof in your land."

For several years my father-in-law was a missionary to the Philippines. My wife told me when she lived in the Philippines that they would receive gift boxes from churches that were filled with items to "help them" in their daily living. In these boxes were Bibles, boxed food, razors and many items which you could use for daily living. She said several times they would receive Bibles that were missing pages or Bibles that were falling apart because people only gave their leftovers. She mentioned one time that they received used razors as a gift from a church for them to use. How sad that people would treat missionaries in such a way.

This is exactly what God was talking about in this verse. God specifically mentioned that when making an offering to Him, be sure that you don't offer Him something that is *"...bruised, or crushed, or broken, or cut..."* What God was teaching His people was don't give God your seconds or rejects. Always offer God your best for God deserves the best.

I am afraid to say that many times people have offered God their seconds and rejects. You ask, "How have we offered God our rejects?" God says in Matthew 25:40, *"...Inasmuch as ye have done it unto one of the least of these my brethren, ye have done it unto me."* When you offer your rejects or seconds to the bus kids, missionaries, pastor's family, the down-and-out of society and to those whom we deem as someone of no importance, according to the Bible you have given that to God.

When making an offering or giving something to someone, always make sure that you are giving to them the same way that you would want others to give to you. A good rule of thumb to live by is this, only offer to God and those whom we consider the least those things which reflect how you want God to bless you. With whatever you give ask yourself this question, "Would I want God to give the same amount and quality to me if He chose to use this gift as the measuring stick to bless me?" I believe if you will ask yourself this question, you will find yourself giving God much better offerings. Remember, you are giving to God when you give to help those in need, so always give your best and never give your rejects or seconds.

The Year of Jubile

Leviticus 25:10

"And ye shall hallow the fiftieth year, and proclaim liberty throughout all the land unto all the inhabitants thereof: it shall be a jubile unto you; and ye shall return every man unto his possession, and ye shall return every man unto his family."

God set up a law for His people stating that every fifty years they were to return to the land of their possession. This year was called the year of jubile. This was an important year as everyone who had sold their inheritance was to go back to their inheritance. Those who had moved away were to move back to the possession and inheritance of their fathers. This year of jubile was important for it caused the children of Israel to remember from whence they came. This year of jubile was a year of re-establishing the borders of their inheritance.

It is interesting to me that God chose every fifty years to celebrate the year of jubile. Interesting in the fact that those fifty years represents each generation. In other words, God wanted each generation to re-establish their inheritance. It was not good enough for the generation to come to live off the convictions and standards of the previous generations. No, each generation was to establish for themselves their inheritance. This thought brings to mind a couple of truths that each of us needs to remember.

First of all, each generation is responsible for what they do with their inheritance. Notice each generation was to re-establish the borders of their inheritance. This is because God wanted each generation to prove to Him that they are worthy of His blessings. Listen, God holds us accountable for what we do with our beliefs. God holds us accountable for what we do with what has been handed to us. We cannot blame previous generations for that which we believe for we are responsible to do right ourselves.

Secondly, each generation will have its own battles to fight for what they believe. Because every fifty years represents a generation, we must realize that every generation will have to fight its battle to establish what they believe. I hear people quite often say they don't want to fight for what they believe because they don't like fighting. I have news for you; God wants each generation to establish what they believe. Each generation will have to establish what they believe about the Bible. Each generation will have to establish what they believe about the local church. Each generation will have to establish their standards. When I say establish what they believe, I mean each generation is responsible to go back to what God wants them to believe not what they want to believe.

I ask you, are you doing your part to establish the right truths for your generation? In your home you are responsible to teach the next generation the right beliefs. In your church you are responsible to defend the fundamentals of the faith. We cannot depend on past generations and think the battles they fought are all over; no, each generation is to fight the battles of re-establishing the borders of what they believe. Let's be sure that our generation establishes the right borders given to us by the Word of God. Let's not fail to fight for these things for the sake of convenience or for the sake of getting along. Let's remember each generation will have to fight its battles; let's not fail in fighting our battles.

Hurt by an Equal

Psalm 55:12

"For it was not an enemy that reproached me; then I could have borne it: neither was it he that hated me that did magnify himself against me; then I would have hid myself from him:"

One of the most unpleasant things I have learned from being in the ministry all these years is that those whom you help the most are the ones who seem to hurt you the most. It would seem that those whom you have helped the most would be the ones who would be the most grateful for what you have done for them, but sadly many times this is not the case.

The Psalmist seems to have the same thing happen to him in this verse. He talked about a person who *"reproached"* him or criticized, blamed and hurt him and how hard it was to take. He said that if it was his enemy who had done this to him he could have taken it for he would expect this from his enemy. But what was hard to take was that the one who reproached him was his friend, the one with whom he had done many things.

Certainly one of the most hurtful things a person can go through in life is when someone close to you turns on you and tries to hurt you. This person may be a sibling, a close friend, your spouse or someone with whom you have worked for years. It is very hard to take when these people turn on you and try to hurt you. Unfortunately this happens way too often. Our first response when the hurt comes is to do exactly what the Psalmist wanted to do and that is to get revenge. Now understand that getting revenge will hurt you more than it will hurt them. Yes, getting revenge may seem sweet at the time, but in the end you will be the one who is hurt the most, for revenge does not take away the bitter feelings inside. When someone close to you has hurt you, you must be careful not to retaliate and try to get even.

The proper response is found in verse 16 as the Psalmist realizes the best way to handle this situation is to call on God and let God be the One Who corrects the problem. When someone has hurt you, I know that your first response is to get even, but instead you must go to the One Who can take care of this problem much better than you can, and that is God. When God handles the problem, He knows best how to deal with the one who has hurt you. Realize that God may handle this problem in such a way that you can still salvage a close relationship. If you try to get revenge, then you may lose that close relationship for life. So, instead of trying to handle the situation yourself, call on God and tell Him about your hurt, and let God be the One Who handles the hurt.

I have no idea what the hurt is that you have gone through, but I know God is the One Who can handle your situation in the best way. Yes, revenge may seem to be the best response, but revenge will hurt you the most. When that one who is near you hurts you, when the disbelief is over and the feelings of revenge are upon you in a great way, then remember to call on God and let Him know how you feel and what you want to do. Then, leave the situation up to God and go on in life realizing God will help you overcome these feelings and will justly deal with the person who has hurt you.

Taking God's Presence for Granted

Numbers 10:34

"And the cloud of the LORD was upon them by day, when they went out of the camp."

What a privilege the children of Israel had to have the presence of God about them daily in the form of a cloud. Everyday these people could wake up and look outside their tents and see the cloud over them and know that God's presence was there with them. Every night these same people could look out their tent doors and see the pillar of fire that had replaced the cloud in the daytime. Imagine at night right before they went to sleep; they could look out and know that God's presence was there with them as they saw the pillar of fire. What a privilege to have God's presence in such a visible way.

Yet, just like normal human beings, the children of Israel got used to having God's presence with them. We can see this in the first verse of chapter eleven when they began to complain about not having any meat to eat. You would think that having God's presence would cause them to feel privileged that God was with them at all times. But, this was not the case as constantly these people either forgot or got used to having God's presence so near.

How careful we as Christians must be that we don't get used to having God's presence in our lives. Let me remind you that if you are a Christian, God's presence dwells inside of you in the form of the Holy Spirit of God. Yes, we think the children of Israel were privileged to have God's visible presence in the form of a cloud or pillar of fire, but Christians have God's presence dwelling IN them. Now let's not get so used to His presence that we allow sin into our lives. Let's not get so used to God's presence that we complain about everything God has provided for us. Let's not get so used to God's presence dwelling in us that we forget to talk to Him daily and acknowledge Him throughout the day.

Yes, as Christians we are privileged to have the presence of God dwelling in us. So, what we ought to do today and everyday is thank God that He dwells in us. Then, we ought to be ever mindful of His presence, and try to please Him in all that we do. Whatever you do, never forget that the presence of God dwells in you. Whatever you do, never take for granted the indwelling presence of an Almighty God.

Nevertheless...

Numbers 13:28

"Nevertheless the people be strong that dwell in the land, and the cities are walled, and very great: and moreover we saw the children of Anak there."

There are some people who no matter how good life is to them it is never good enough. Everybody knows someone like this. This is the person who, when asked how they are doing, is still telling you twenty minutes later how they are doing. Yet, when you hear how "bad" their life is, and see what all they have, you shake your head at why they are complaining.

In this chapter, the children of Israel were commanded by God to go into the land of Canaan to spy out the land and bring a report back to the people as to what this land was like. When the twelve spies came back, ten spies had an evil report and two had a good report. You notice that the ten spies talked briefly about how good the land was, but they followed up in this verse with the word, *"Nevertheless."* Amazing to say the least! Here they are about ready to go into a wonderful land, and the only thing they could see was the walled cities, strong armies and giants.

I find this is how many people are today. God can bless people and give them blessings far beyond what they deserve, and yet all they can talk about is what is not going good. You have people who are members of great churches, and yet the only thing they talk about is the negative they see in their church. In America, people have been blessed beyond measure, and yet all you hear from the majority of people is how bad they have it. It's about time people stop giving the "nevertheless" speech and recognize that God has been mighty good to them in every area of their lives.

Let me ask you, are you a person who is always saying like the children of Israel, "Nevertheless?" In your marriage, do you have a wonderful spouse who has been faithful to you, and yet all you do is talk about the "nevertheless?" Teenager, do you have parents who love you and care for you and yet all you can do is talk about the "nevertheless?" We could go on and on talking about our church, place of employment, the country in which we live, or the school you attend. In all of these areas most people have a pretty good thing going, and yet when you talk to them all they want to talk about is the "nevertheless" subjects.

Be careful in your life that you don't become a person who talks about the "nevertheless." Don't be the one who always sees the bad in every circumstance for that is the "nevertheless" that I am talking about. In your life, be like the two spies who came back with the good report of what God was about ready to give to them. It is a choice to be either of these two things. Choose to be the person who sees the good in life and life will be much more enjoyable to live. Not only will it be more enjoyable to live, but you will be a person who will be more enjoyable to be around. People like being around a person who sees the good in life.

A Governed Spirit

Proverbs 25:28

"He that hath no rule over his own spirit is like a city that is broken down, and without walls."

One of the more difficult things a person achieves in life is that of governing their own spirit. God likens the person who does not rule or govern their spirit like a city that is broken and defenseless. Notice, God said the man who doesn't *"...rule his own spirit is like a city that is broken down..."* In other words this person who doesn't have control of his spirit has a life that is broken, or to put it plainly, not working. When you don't control your own spirit, you are wasting your time in life because you have a life that is broken. A broken life is definitely not going to be used to fix the lives of others.

But going even further, the person who doesn't have control of his spirit is defenseless. Defenseless from what? Defenseless from allowing others to control what gets him up and what gets him down. In other words, the person who is not ruling his spirit is completely at the mercy of whatever the outside circumstance is that does control his spirit. Now the key to living a life that works and is under control is to control and rule your own spirit.

One of the ways you can rule and govern your own spirit is to study yourself and find out what gets you up and what gets you down. I have said this several times, make a study of yourself and find out what in life causes you to get down and what causes you to get up. How can you rule your spirit if you don't know what depresses you and what encourages you? The key to ruling your spirit is knowing how to avoid what attacks your spirit and how to access that which encourages your spirit. Then, once you know what gets your spirit up and down, avoid that which brings your spirit down and do whatever causes your spirit to get up.

Ruling your own spirit is done on purpose. Ruling your spirit is done by performing actions that keep your spirit up. If you know what gets you up then do it. If you know what gets you down then avoid it. Simply be the ruler that governs your spirit.

One last thing, if you are going to rule your spirit then you must not let outside sources control you. What I am talking about is be careful about letting people dictate what your spirit ought to be like. There are some people out there who are spirit killers. Avoid them like the plague! If you rule your spirit then you must not let into the kingdom of your spirit those who would rule it by their wrong influence. I must be in total control of my own spirit, and one way I do this is by controlling who I am around. If someone that I know always gets my spirit down whenever I talk to them or get around them, then I am going to avoid them so I can be in control of my own spirit.

One of the greatest accomplishments you will achieve in life is that of ruling and governing your spirit. When the day comes that outside circumstances and other people do not control whether your spirit is up, then that is the day you will be in control of your life. Always remember this, he who rules his spirit rules his life!

What's Your Excuse This Time?

Proverbs 26:13

"The slothful man saith, There is a lion in the way; a lion is in the streets."

In the Book of Proverbs God describes different types of people to help teach us what we should become or what we should not become. One of the types of people whom God describes is the slothful person. Most definitely this is one of the types of people whom we don't want to be like. The word *"slothful"* means "sluggish, lazy, idle or indolent." There is nothing good that can be said about the slothful person. This person, though they may not live a wicked life, will destroy themselves by their actions, or should I say lack of action.

Notice one of the ways God describes the slothful person in verse 13. The slothful person always has an excuse for why they can't do something. In this verse his excuse was there was a lion in the streets. How silly it is to give an excuse like this. Most likely there was not a lion in the streets, but the slothful person used that as an excuse for not doing anything. Slothful people always have an excuse for why they cannot do something. Yet it is interesting that others face the same problems but they are still able to do what they are supposed to do.

Every person needs to be careful about always having an excuse for why they are not able to do what they are supposed to do. Listen, responsibility is never easy and at times it won't be pleasant, but we still must fulfill our obligations. The slothful person will find an excuse to get out of their responsibilities. For instance, the slothful person says they don't have time to do what they are supposed to do. They supposedly are too busy to fulfill their responsibilities.

The slothful person many times will try to use health as their excuse. For instance, it is amazing they are always sick when it is time to perform that for which they are responsible. My question to them is this, can't you work when you are sick? The slothful person will even talk about how busy they are just to get out of doing something. The amazing thing about this person is nobody else sees all they claim that they are doing.

Be careful about finding excuses to get out of doing things. Be careful about avoiding work or responsibility because you always have something that conflicts. If you don't want to be labeled as slothful, then instead of finding excuses, find a way to do what you are supposed to do. Our nation is slowly dying because of the slothfulness we find in the workplace. Don't be a contributor to the slothfulness of this nation.

Every Christian should be diligent. Every Christian should be known as a hard worker. No Christian should ever be labeled as slothful. Let's be sure we don't take on the characteristics of the slothful and use excuses for not accomplishing tasks and responsibilities. Instead, let's find ways to accomplish those tasks and fulfill our responsibilities.

Wholly Followed

Numbers 32:11

"Surely none of the men that came up out of Egypt, from twenty years old and upward, shall see the land which I sware unto Abraham, unto Isaac, and unto Jacob; because they have not wholly followed me:"

The greatest commentary on the Bible is the Bible. We read in this verse the story of the twelve spies who went into the land of Canaan to search out the land. The Bible teaches us that ten of the spies came back with an evil report while two came back with a good report. But when we come to this verse, we find the sin which angered God so much was that these men did not wholly follow God.

The word *"wholly"* means "entirely, completely, with all the parts." This verse did not say these men did not follow God, it said these men did not follow God wholly, with all of their being. I find then what God wants from us is to follow Him wholly. A Christian who may follow God, but not wholly follow Him, is a Christian who angers God. There are three areas in which I find that God wants us to wholly follow Him.

First, we need to wholly follow God with our actions. These men who went to search out the Land of Canaan were following God with their actions, but only up to a certain point. This is the problem many Christians have in following God, they will follow Him with their actions up to a certain point, then they stop following. God demands complete followship! He demands that we wholly, entirely and with all of our being follow Him with our actions.

There is a second way we are to follow God and that is with our heart. This is interesting in the fact that sometimes you will find people follow God with their actions, but their heart is not following God. It is like a child who obeys their parents, but inside, they are rebelling and don't want to do what their parents tell them to do. When God demands us to wholly follow Him, He also demands our heart to follow Him as well. Yes your outward actions may be following God, but your heart may be following the world or your own desires. To God this is nothing less than disobedience. You may have the actions to prove you are following God, but is your heart wholly following God as well? Your heart involves your emotions which means God wants both your physical actions and emotions to be involved in following Him.

There is one other area where these men failed to follow God and that was in their faith. They did not have the faith that God could knock down the walls or defeat the giants in this land. When God demands that we wholly follow Him, He wants us to follow Him with our actions, our heart, and even our faith to wholly follow Him. This is where many Christians fall short! They follow Him with their actions and even with their heart, but when it comes time to step out by faith and follow Him, they stop at this point. You will never please God until by faith you wholly follow Him. When God asks you to step out by faith, though you may not see how God can perform what He asks you to do, God expects complete obedience in following Him with your faith.

Are you wholly following God? Are you following Him with your actions, heart and faith? Caleb and Joshua wholly followed God, and He blessed them. Likewise, if you will wholly follow God in these areas He will bless you too.

Encourage Him

Deuteronomy 1:38

"But Joshua the son of Nun, which standeth before thee, he shall go in thither: encourage him: for he shall cause Israel to inherit it."

Jealousy is a horrible sin. When a person becomes jealous of someone else, they are upset when they see good happen to that person. Most of the time jealousy happens because someone has the character to do something that you find yourself lacking.

One of the people in the Bible who could have had a reason to be jealous was Moses. We read here in this verse that Moses was not going to be able to go into the Promised Land because of the sin of smiting the rock to which God told him to speak in order for water to come out. To add insult to injury, God told Moses to prepare Joshua to take the children of Israel into the Promised Land. Can you imagine the jealousy that could have creeped into the heart of Moses to see someone else have something he could not have? Not only did God command Moses to prepare Joshua to lead His people into the Promised Land, but God also told Moses to encourage him. This command by God could have been a two-edged sword to Moses if jealousy ruled his life, but instead it became a motivation for the rest of Moses' life to train and encourage someone else to do something that he would never be able to do.

I find many people who lack the character of Moses in being able to encourage someone who is able to do something they are not able to do. I find most of the time, instead of encouraging these people, we try to set up traps to cause them to fail or discourage them in those things which we wish we could do hoping this will cause them to fail. Be careful of becoming this type of a person. Just because a person can lose weight and you can't, you should not discourage them, but instead you should continue to encourage them. Just because a person has character to continue to do something that you find yourself not being able to do that does not give you a right to try and stop them from doing whatever this is.

We should find ourselves happy that people are able to accomplish something that we are not able to do. We should be thrilled that people hold a position which we are not able to hold. In your life, whomever it is that you find yourself jealous or envious of; one thing you can do is encourage them to continue doing this action or task. When you find yourself encouraging them and they succeed, you can take heart in the fact that you are part of the reason for their success. Put away jealousy and envy and strive to be the ultimate encourager of those who are able to do things which you cannot do.

God Delivered

Deuteronomy 3:3

"So the LORD our God delivered into our hands Og also, the king of Bashan, and all his people: and we smote him until none was left to him remaining."

To remind the children of Israel that God is a God Whom you can trust, Moses told the story of God commanding Israel to take Bashan. God made the statement in verse 2, *"...Fear him not: for I will deliver him, and all his people, and his land, into thy hand..."* We then see in verse 3, *"So the LORD our God delivered into our hand Og also, the king of Bashan, and all his people..."* When God told Israel to go and take this city, God delivered on His promise and helped them defeat the king and the city.

God is always a God Who will deliver on His Word. Though we live in a day when a person's word does not mean that much, one thing you can bank on is that God ALWAYS delivers on His Word. If God tells you to do something and that He will come through to help you, you can count on it that God will deliver on His promise. O, there may be times when you wonder if God is going to come through, but God always comes through.

I like to remind people that God is rarely early, never late, but always on time. There have been many times in my life when I was beginning to sweat hoping that God would deliver on His promise, and each time God delivered on His promises to me. In all these years of living by faith, when it came time for the need to be met, God delivered His promise to me. In my entire life, I have never had to stand up and tell a people or an individual that God did not come through. In my entire life, I have never heard a person stand up and say God did not come through, because God is a God Who will deliver on His promise.

Christian, you may at this very moment be wondering if God is going to come through in your life; let me give you hope that God will deliver on His promise if you are obeying Him. Christian, if you are scared to step out by faith and obey God in an area that may seem frightening, let me remind you that God will always deliver on His promise to you to be there for you when you step out by faith. All you need to do is go through the Bible and look at how God came through and delivered on His promises for His people, and realize that He has not changed and will deliver for you as well.

Whatever it is today that you are concerned with, take courage in the fact that God will deliver His promise just for you like He has done for others. Just step out and trust God, and I promise you that God will deliver.

God's Boot Camp

Deuteronomy 8:2

"And thou shalt remember all the way which the LORD thy God led thee these forty years in the wilderness, to humble thee, and to prove thee, to know what was in thine heart, whether thou wouldest keep his commandments, or no."

Each of the stages that the children of Israel went through has a comparison to the Christian life. For instance, coming out of Egypt is a type of salvation. Crossing over of the Red Sea was a type of separation from the world. The wilderness is the testing ground or boot camp of God to prepare us for His perfect will for our life which is the Promised Land.

We learn in this verse that when God sent the children of Israel through the wilderness, He guided them through all their victories and difficulties. He did this for three reasons: to humble them, prove them, and to find out what was in their hearts. God does these same thing to us to prepare us for the perfect will for which He made us. We need to learn that from the time of salvation to the time when God places us in His perfect will, He will guide us through victories and trials to prepare us for that perfect will. Simply put, the wilderness is the boot camp to prepare us for the war of God's perfect will.

In God's boot camp, the first reason God puts us through hard times is to humble us. We are naturally proud. Because of this, God must humble us in order for Him to be able to use us. Just as a recruit has his head shaved at boot camp to humble him, God likewise wants to take our pride away so that He can teach us. As long as we have pride in our hearts we are unteachable and God cannot use us to the capacity to which He desires. So to bring us to the point of usefulness, God must send hard times and trials our way to humble us.

The second reason God sends us through hard times is to get all the impurities out of our life so that we can be a better soldier for Him. The word *"prove"* is the same word that a refiner uses to purify the gold that he puts through the fire. God sends us through the fire to take out the impurities in our life in order to prepare us for His perfect will. Yes, the fire is unpleasant, but the fire refines us and makes us into the Christian soldier God has in mind that we become. Without these hard times, God cannot make us into a better Christian. The hard times of the wilderness are there for God to make us better soldiers for Him.

The final reason for the hard times that God allows is to find out what it will take for us to stop serving Him. When the soldier goes through boot camp, those hard times during boot camp will tell the drill instructor what it will take to make the soldier quit. God needs to know before He places us in His perfect will what it will take to get us to quit. The hard times of the wilderness show what kind of determination is in our heart. During these times there is nothing wrong with wanting to quit, but it is wrong to quit. No matter how hard our situation may be, WE MUST NOT QUIT!

God's perfect will should be the goal for all of us. We must remember, before God will allow us into His perfect will for our lives, He must send us through the spiritual boot camp of the wilderness. As you go through this boot camp, let God's boot camp accomplish the work that God intended for it to do in you. Let this boot camp humble you, make you better and prove to God that you are worthy of His perfect will because you won't quit when hard times come. Strive to graduate from God's boot camp of the wilderness so you can live in the perfect will He has for you.

Response to Disgruntled Church Members

Deuteronomy 17:2

"If there be found among you, within any of thy gates which the LORD thy God giveth thee, man or woman, that hath wrought wickedness in the sight of the LORD thy God, in transgressing his covenant,"

In the matter of a person committing wickedness in the congregation of Israel, God was very explicit how His people should deal with such a person. The wickedness that God was talking about is explained in the next verse which is a person serving or worshipping another god. God said when a person did this, they were to be stoned to death and put out of the congregation of Israel. God wanted His people to be very careful about letting associations destroy their walk with God. Though this truth was God instituting the laws for the children of Israel, I believe we can learn a valuable lesson in how to handle people who have left fellowship with us in our churches.

I have recently helped several pastors who have lost church members because of disloyalty. In each of these cases those who left took people with them which hurt the church. The one thing people must be careful about when a person leaves a church is that we don't let this person ruin our spirit about our church and cause us to also leave. We must learn, as God taught us in this verse, to stop fellowship with this person. Now I am not saying we ought to be rude to the person, but for the sake of our spirit staying right we must not fellowship with those who have left our church for a wrong reason.

The common statement you hear when this happens is that this person is their friend. This may be true, but you must understand that this person is the one who changed, not you. Normally what a person like this will do with you is they will say, "You're still going to be my friend even though I leave, right?" They try to pass the guilt upon you for their wrong. Now you must realize they are the ones who have left. It is their heart that has changed and not yours. For them to say something like this to you is nothing more than selfishness, which is only an extension of the reason why they left your church anyway. You must remember when something like this happens they are the ones who have made the move. Because they moved, it was their action that moved themselves into a different relationship with you.

We must learn, as God teaches us in this verse, that when people leave fellowship with our congregation for the wrong reason, for the sake of our spirit and walk with God, we must not fellowship with them any more. Yes, be kind and courteous to them when you see them. No, we should not talk about them in a bad way in our church after they have left. Yes, we should pray that God will work in their hearts to bring them back to us. But for the sake of our walk with God being what it should be, we must not continue to fellowship with those who have left for the wrong reason. If we do, we will end up making the same move they made. Let's be careful about our associations with those who have left our churches for the wrong reason. Let's pray for them and love them, but let's cut our fellowship with them for the sake of preserving our spirit regarding our church.

Wisdom's Silence

Proverbs 1:28
"Then shall they call upon me, but I will not answer; they shall seek me early, but they shall not find me:"

One of the greatest problems I have seen in people is they let life pass right by them and never study the lessons of life which are all around them. People simply forget the happenings of life when they should have learned from each happening that they have seen.

The Book of Proverbs has been called a book full of wisdom. In the very first chapter of this book God said that wisdom calls out to the simple. God said that wisdom cries out in the street, in the place of business, in the entrance to the gates of the city, and in every instance of life wisdom cries with a loud voice. The problem with most is their ears are deaf to the voice of wisdom. She cries, but no one listens. She pleads for people to hear her, but her voice is silenced by the affairs of our life. God said in the verse above that one day you will call for wisdom, but she will not answer. You will seek early for wisdom, and she will not be found. The reason why is because God already placed the path of wisdom in front of you at an earlier time of life and you never took time to learn the wisdom that you needed. Then the day came when you could have used that wisdom, but because you did not take the time to learn from wisdom when she was there to teach you, mistakes were made in your life.

To make this as simple as I can, every situation of life that has come your way is there to teach you for some future purpose. Many times God allows us to see things in life so we can learn from them something to use in the future. On the job we see things happen so we can learn from them to use in the future. In the church we are allowed to see things happen so we can help others in the future. In people's lives we were allowed to see the mistakes they've made so that we don't make the same mistakes. Over and over again in our daily life we see things that are placed in our pathway for us to learn so we can use that wisdom later.

Now you must be careful not to let these times of teachings pass by without learning something from them. Things happen every day of your life from which you can learn. Whenever you see these situations happen in your life or someone else's life, stop and learn from those situations. God did not allow these to happen in your presence for no reason at all. He allowed them to happen so you can learn from them to help you in the future.

Most wise people are not wise by accident; they are wise because they learned from every situation in life. If you are not careful, wisdom will become silent in your life because she was already in your presence at an earlier time and you did not learn from her. Be aware of everything that happens in life, and learn from it. Don't get so busy that you don't learn from each and every instance of life. God allows these things to happen in your presence so you can learn. Be sure that you learn from those situations so that, when the day comes when you call out to wisdom, wisdom will respond because you learned from her at an earlier time.

If Thou Wilt Not Hearken...

Deuteronomy 28:15

"But it shall come to pass, if thou wilt not hearken unto the voice of the LORD thy God, to observe to do all his commandments and his statutes which I command thee this day; that all these curses shall come upon thee, and overtake thee:"

When you read this chapter of the book of Deuteronomy, it would seem that the blessings of God are not as great as the punishment of God when you disobey Him. There is a reason for this which I will explain in a moment, but before I do, let me point out to you a statement that God made very early in the chapter. In Deuteronomy 28:2 God said, *"And all these blessings shall come on thee, and overtake thee..."* When God's blessings come upon your life, you will notice that God said these blessings will overtake you. In other words, His blessings will be so numerous that there will be no way to hold them all. What a promise God gives to us for doing right!

On the other hand, when we do wrong the punishment of God will be great and overtake us as well. I believe the reason why God stresses how severe His punishment will be in this chapter is because when you experience the punishment of God, it will seem far worse than all the blessings which God has given you. Though this is not the case, God's punishment for our sins is severe! God demands of His people to obey His commandments. If they do, He will bless them more than they can handle. If they don't, His punishment will seem to outweigh all the blessings which have come upon our lives.

Does it seem to you that more bad has come into your life than good? Does it seem like God's blessings in your life are not as numerous as the punishment you have received from Him? If this be the case, then what you ought to do is find out the reason that God saw fit to punish you. What you ought to do is search your heart and life and find out the cause of His punishment on your life. Instead of griping about how "God does not love you," what you should be doing is searching for the cause of His punishment. Most likely you know the cause, but you just don't want to stop doing what is causing the punishment. God does not send His punishment to hurt you, but to bring you back to Him so He can bless you with blessings that will overtake you.

Let's be diligent in our lives to get rid of sin. Let's always remember that God would rather bless us than punish us. The choice is ours; so ultimately, the result is our choice as well. Let's choose God's blessings by living right!

Nothing Between

Deuteronomy 30:20

"That thou mayest love the LORD thy God, and that thou mayest obey his voice, and that thou mayest cleave unto him: for he is thy life, and the length of thy days: that thou mayest dwell in the land which the LORD sware unto thy fathers, to Abraham, to Isaac, and to Jacob, to give them."

When Moses came to the end of his life, he gave a final warning to the people of God. One of those warnings we find in this verse, *"...That thou mayest love the LORD thy God, and that thou mayest obey his voice, and that thou mayest cleave unto him..."* Notice that last warning, *"...that thou mayest cleave unto him..."* Moses was warning the people that they needed to cleave unto the LORD.

The word *"cleave"* means "to unite or be united so closely in interest or affection." I like to put it this way, get so close to whatever you're holding onto that nothing can get between you and that object.

In the Bible, God commands us to cleave to two things, our spouse and the LORD. Other than these two things, nothing else in life truly matters. Truthfully, if you would cleave to your spouse and the LORD, your life would be in the right order. All the problems that come into our life come from letting something in between one of these two areas.

As I thought of cleaving unto the LORD, two things came to mind that I believe will be a help to you. First, when God says to cleave unto the LORD, I believe one thing He is teaching us is to cleave for our life. I picture it as a person holding onto a rope for dear life so that they don't plunge to their death. I believe in life we need to hold onto the LORD for dear life realizing that if we let go of Him we will plunge to our spiritual death.

Secondly, we should cleave so tightly to the LORD that nothing comes between us and the Saviour. My mind goes to the song, "Nothing between my soul and the Saviour..." Oh, how I long in my life, and you should as well, that nothing comes between the Saviour and me. Cleave so tight to the LORD that no person gets between you and the Saviour. Cleave so tight to the LORD that no sin comes between you and the Saviour. Cleave so tight to the LORD that no desire comes between you and the Saviour. Cleave so tight to the LORD that NOTHING comes between you and the Saviour.

As you read this devotional, I ask you, is there ANYTHING between you and the Saviour? Have you loosened your grip on the LORD and something in your life has come between you and Him? Whatever it is that has come between you and the LORD, get it out! Cleave so tight to the LORD that nothing can get between you and Him. Make it your goal in life to say there is nothing between my soul and the Saviour.

A Sanctified People

Joshua 3:5

"And Joshua said unto the people, Sanctify yourselves: for to morrow the LORD will do wonders among you."

Joshua made a statement in this verse which is the key to serving God successfully in every area of the Christian life. The statement he made was, *"...Sanctify yourselves..."* The only chance a Christian has in serving God throughout his entire life is to sanctify him. The word *"sanctify"* means *"to set apart for a specific purpose."* In other words, if a Christian is going to be successful in serving God, they must set themselves apart to serve God. The family that is going to be a godly family must sanctify themselves, or set themselves apart for the purpose of serving God. The business that wants to be a business that glorifies God must set itself apart to glorify God. The life that wants to serve God and glorify Him with its existence must sanctify itself for that purpose. Just like an athlete sets himself apart for the purpose of his sport, a Christian must set themselves apart for the purpose of serving God. If this is going to be done then a few things must be accomplished in order to achieve sanctification.

First of all you will notice that you are the one to sanctify yourself. Joshua commanded the people to sanctify themselves, and if you are going to serve God, you must decide to sanctify yourself. A person will never be successful in setting themselves apart for God's service without first deciding to do so.

Secondly, if you are going to be sanctified for the purpose of serving God, you must sacrifice some things in order to accomplish this. Again, like an athlete sets himself apart for the sake of his sport, this athlete many times will sacrifice things that he normally would partake of all for the sake of his sport. Likewise a Christian who wants to be successful in his service to God must sacrifice certain things in order to be successful. Not everything that we sacrifice will be wrong to do, but we will never be as successful without setting some things aside all for the purpose of serving God. Too many times we say that something is not wrong, and we are right, but for the sake of accomplishing what we are trying to accomplish, we must sacrifice that desire to do a work for God.

Last of all, sanctification is not a one-time act; it is something that must be done daily. To be successful serving God, we must set ourselves apart daily for His service. Without a daily sanctification, we will never have a life filled with service to God.

Realize every day you live that you are the one who must decide to set yourself apart to serve God that day. Then, realize that if you are going to be successful that day in serving God, you must sacrifice some things in order to accomplish your service that day. Last of all remember, yesterday's sanctification of your life does not apply to today; you must set yourself apart daily to serve God. Then, and only then, will you be a sanctified person.

So Did Joshua

Joshua 11:15

"As the LORD commanded Moses his servant, so did Moses command Joshua, and so did Joshua; he left nothing undone of all that the LORD commanded Moses."

God's commandments never change! Just because society changes does not mean that God changes! God is a god Who never changes; therefore, His Word and His commandments never change. If God commanded us to do something 100 years ago, He still commands us today to do the same thing. His commandments do not change to fit man's lifestyle. God expects us to change to fit His commandments.

If God's commandments never change, and they don't, then we need to make sure we hand down to the next generation these commandments. In fact, we are commanded by God to hand down to the next generation the commandments that He has given to us.

In this verse, we see exactly how it is handed to the next generation. I want you to notice that the LORD commanded Moses. Then in the next phrase we see Moses commanded and taught Joshua those same commandments. Then the last thing we see is Joshua followed the commandments that originally came from God. Now if Joshua didn't want liberalism to creep into Israel, he needed to hand down to the next generation the same commands which he followed.

The best way we can keep our churches, children and the next generation from going liberal is to keep doing what we are commanded to do. I have found the best teacher of God's commands is our actions. If we will just keep preaching the Word of God in our churches, soul winning, upholding the personal standards of the Bible and all that God commands us to do, then our churches will not go liberal. The same can be said about our homes. If mom and dad will keep going to church, keep praying together as a family, keep reading and memorizing from the King James Bible and keep the standards of personal separation in our homes, then we have a better chance of our children not going liberal.

My question to you is this, are you following God's commandments so that the next generation that follows you will know what those commandments are? Your children and church will only keep doing right if you keep doing right. The best way to fight liberalism is to keep doing what God commands us to do. We can say we hate liberalism and compromise, but if we are not following all of God's commandments, then we are contributing to the compromise of our children and church. Take a personal inspection of your life and be sure that you are following the commands of God's Word that have been handed down to you.

Unwavering Strength for War

Joshua 14:11

"As yet I am as strong this day as I was in the day that Moses sent me: as my strength was then, even so is my strength now, for war, both to go out, and to come in."

Caleb was 85 years of age when he approached Moses about land that he wanted as his inheritance. As he talked to Moses he made the statement, *"...as my strength was then, even so is my strength now, for war, both to go out, and to come in."* At first glance you would think that Caleb was saying that he still had the strength at 85 years of age that he had when he was 40 years of age, but this is not what he was talking about. Caleb was saying that at 85 years of age he had not lost the stomach for fighting wars that he had when he was 40 years of age. Notice the verse says, *"...so is my strength now, for war..."* Age did not wear Caleb down to the point that he would not fight.

I point this out because normally the older a person gets the less they want to fight for right. Recently I was talking to a preacher who was in the upper part of his middle-aged years of life and he made the statement to me that he was just too old to fight certain battles. First of all, I never have found in the Bible where a person becomes too old to stand and fight for truth.

Secondly, when truth is attacked we need the gray heads to show the younger generation how to stand and fight for truth. I have observed many preachers who once stood for something when they were younger who are not willing to fight for what they used to stand for all because they no longer have the stomach to fight.

Christian, as distasteful as it is to fight battles, we must never come to the point where we are not willing to jump into a battle for truth and right. Truth is always worth standing and fighting for. The problem is that the older you get the more you know about what it takes to fight a battle. Because you know what it takes to fight a battle, you really don't want to have to go through the hardships and heartaches of battles once again. As distasteful as fighting a battle for truth is, we must never grow too old to fight for truth.

Let's be sure that even if we are an older person, as Caleb who at age 85 was willing to go conquer a land, that we don't let up in the fight for truth. Whether this fight is fought through soul winning, teaching a Sunday school class, preaching the Word of God, or even having to fight fellow brethren who are trying to bring in false doctrine, let's always realize the battle for truth must be fought regardless of age. If you are a senior person don't stand on the sidelines watching others do what you should be doing. Jump in and get involved with the fight yourself. Those of us who are younger need to see an older generation who have already fought battles show us how to fight by fighting battles today. I say to you as the song says, "Stand up, stand up for Jesus, ye soldiers of the cross..."

The LORD was with Judah

Judges 1:19

"And the LORD was with Judah; and he drave out the inhabitants of the mountain; but could not drive out the inhabitants of the valley, because they had chariots of iron."

One of the most desirable statements in the Bible is said about the tribe of Judah. In this verse the statement was made, *"And the LORD was with Judah..."* I don't know of anything that a Christian could want more than God being with them. Every time you see that God is with someone, great things happen in their lives. Every time the LORD was with Samson, he did mighty works for the LORD. God was with Samuel, and he became one of the great prophets of old. God was with Joseph, and the Bible said he became prosperous. The LORD was obviously with David when he conquered Goliath. God was with Gideon, and he ended up conquering the great Midianite army. The LORD was with Joshua, and he led the children of Israel into the Promised Land. Over and over again we see that when the LORD was with someone, great things happened in that person's life or in their nation.

The greatest need today in our society is for people to have the LORD with them. Whatever the problem you face today, it can be solved if you have the LORD with you. If the LORD was with a married couple in their marriage, I promise you, there would be no strife in the home. If a church had the LORD with them, great things would happen in that city. If an individual had the LORD with them, as seen in the instances above, great things would be accomplished.

More than you need money; you need the LORD with you. More than you need a new house or car; you need the LORD with you. More than you need that promotion on the job; you need the LORD with you. More than you need whatever it is that you think you need; you need the LORD with you.

Your prayer and desire for today ought to be to ask the LORD to be with you in ALL that you do. Everyday before you start your day, ask the LORD to be with you throughout the day. Then as you go through your day, whisper a prayer to the LORD and ask Him to be with you as you do your daily tasks. When you have the LORD with you, as Romans 8:31 says, *"...who can be against us?"* The answer for victory in your life is having the LORD with you.

Again

Judges 3:12

"And the children of Israel did evil again in the sight of the LORD: and the LORD strengthened Eglon the king of Moab against Israel, because they had done evil in the sight of the LORD."

Over and over again in the book of Judges God made the statement about the children of Israel that they did evil again in His sight. The pattern of Israel was: do right; when the leader died they did wrong; God punished them for their sin; because of this punishment they came back to God. This seemed to be the pattern of these people. How sad that they fell into a pattern where it is said that they did evil again.

Everybody normally lives their life in cycles. As long as I have been in the ministry, I have learned to study people and find out what their cycle is to determine their degree of usefulness. The statement that a tiger never loses its stripes is so true because I have seen people do wrong, then do right to only come back and do wrong again. This is their pattern!

Let me ask you, what is your pattern? If anybody should know what your pattern in your life is, you should certainly know what you are apt to do again. Is your pattern do right, then do wrong, then do right to only go back and do wrong again? Is your pattern simply doing wrong all the time? Or, is your pattern the best pattern of doing right all the time? The latter should be your goal.

If you are like the children of Israel who were prone to go back to doing wrong, then you need to break that pattern. People who live their lives doing right, wrong, right and wrong again are people whose potential for doing great things for God is very limited. Breaking this pattern is a choice that only you can make. As long as you use excuses as your crutch to hold you to this pattern, you will never break that bad pattern. Your goal in life ought to be to be known as a person who is doing right again. This should be the ultimate goal of every Christian.

If your pattern is the same as the children of Israel's, then decide today to break that pattern with God's help, and become known as a person who does right again. If you are a person who is known for doing right again, then ask God to help you never to break that pattern in your life. Work hard at guarding a good pattern so that throughout your life you can be known as a person who did right again.

Hurray for Jephthah's Daughter

Judges 11:39

"And it came to pass at the end of two months, that she returned unto her father, who did with her according to his vow which he had vowed: and she knew no man. And it was a custom in Israel,"

When you read the story of Jephthah, I think we miss a truth that would be helpful to many people. I can't help but think of myself and my daughter Caitlyn as I read this story. The reason why is because Jephthah's daughter was his only child. I can understand exactly how much he cared for his little girl. Yet, when he made the vow to God that he would offer the first thing that met him when he came home from the battle, I am confident that he did not think his daughter would be the one to meet him. I can only imagine the heartbreak that he experienced when he saw his daughter come out to meet him.

Yet, let me praise the daughter of Jephthah a bit. As I look at this story, I see a young lady who every young lady should strive to emulate. Let me show you a few things about this young lady.

First of all, she made her dad one of her best friends. In verse 34 you see that when her dad came home from the battle, she came running out to meet him. I believe this young lady was most likely in her teenage years, and she still was very close to her dad. I know when I come home from my trips and my daughter Caitlyn is home; she is always the first one out the door to welcome her dad home from a revival meeting. This always thrills my heart! But let me say, I hope she continues this well into her teenage years. Young ladies should not grow apart from their dad the older they get;

instead, they should grow closer to their dad because he is there to protect and love them.

The second thing you will notice about this young lady is that she was a spiritual young lady. When realizing that her dad had made a vow, she told her dad that he should keep the vow even though it meant her life would be taken from her. Let me tell you, it takes someone spiritual to say this. I wonder if this were you, would you have had the same response, or would you have told your father that this was a dumb vow to make? She, being a spiritual young lady, knew the importance of keeping a vow to God. Every person who reads this should realize the importance of keeping vows to God. Spiritual people will keep the vows they make to God!

Thirdly, she was pure! In this story we see that she died a virgin. I believe this is something noteworthy to talk about. Every young person should strive to remain a virgin until the day they are married. This is a worthy goal and a godly goal as well. Though our society has tried to make this a dirty word, it takes more strength to remain a virgin than it does to be loose like most of society is today.

Last of all, she was a young lady who had integrity. She did right even to her own detriment which shows integrity. Let me tell you, our society needs an old-fashioned dose of integrity. We need people who are like this young lady who even if right hurts them, they still do what is right.

I close by saying hurray for the daughter of Jephthah. If only we could fill our churches once again with young ladies like Jephthah's daughter! Better yet, we all should strive as well, whether man or woman, to be like this young lady in our daily lives.

Running with the Enemy

Judges 16:5

"And the lords of the Philistines came up unto her, and said unto her, Entice him, and see wherein his great strength lieth, and by what means we may prevail against him, that we may bind him to afflict him: and we will give thee every one of us eleven hundred pieces of silver."

We have heard, and know, that you can never deal with terrorists. This whole reason why you cannot deal with them, negotiate with them or converse with them is because their only desire is to kill and destroy you.

Samson never learned this valuable lesson. Throughout the life of Samson we see him running with the enemy. He dated the daughters of the enemy; he went to social events of the enemy; he made companions with the enemy; he even married one of the young ladies of the enemy. At the end of his life, you see that the enemy took his life with a great show of strength in the Philistine temple. In the verse above we see the goal of the Philistines, the enemy of Samson, was to bind him and afflict him. This was their whole goal throughout his life, and he never saw that this is what the enemy wanted to do with him.

Christian, our enemy is Satan, sin, and the world. You must grasp the fact that you can never negotiate with these, for they only desire to destroy everything that you believe in. You cannot make deals with Satan without him binding you and afflicting you for the rest of your life. You cannot negotiate with your sin thinking that your sin will do nothing to affect you. No, your sin will eventually bind you and afflict you for the rest of your life.

SPIRITUAL ESPRESSO VOL 3

The world is not the friend of the Christian or the church. Yet, we see quite often churches compromising their stand thinking that if they let down a little bit that the world will get along with them. Let me be very blunt; the goal of the world is to completely destroy every church and every belief of Christianity. They may even tell us if we will let up in one area that we can all get along. But just like a terrorists, when you give in to the world, you will find the world NEVER follows through with their end of the bargain. The reason is because they only want one thing, to destroy the church and all Christian beliefs.

I say all of this to warn you that compromise with the world should never be an option for the Christian or the church. We must understand the only thing they want is for us to be gone. Therefore, let's stand for what we believe in and not let up. Let's not sit down at the negotiating table with sin. Sin and compromise will bind us and afflict us for the rest of our lives. Let's be Christians who are aware that the world has never liked the church or Christians, and this will never change. Let's be strong and decide that compromising our stand and what we believe in is never an option. The only option the church and the Christian has is to do what the Bible commands, for this is where true freedom lies.

Ruth Clave Unto Her

Ruth 1:14

"And they lifted up their voice, and wept again: and Orpah kissed her mother in law; but Ruth clave unto her."

When you study the life of Ruth, there are many good attributes about this lady that could and should be talked about. One of the greatest attributes I find about Ruth is that she was a true friend. At this point in the story you read how Naomi came to Orpah and Ruth and told them to go on back home to their gods and people for she had nothing to offer them. Naomi was very blunt in the fact that she was a widow, and even if she were to get married again, she was too old to have another son. We find at this point that Orpah went back to her people, but Ruth clave to Naomi. This was true friendship for Naomi had nothing to offer Ruth. In fact, you read in Ruth 1:21 how Naomi had nothing left of lands or money. She put it this way, *"I went out full, and the LORD hath brought me home again empty..."* Though Naomi had nothing to offer, Ruth still understood that friendship is not based on opportunity, friendship is based on the fact that once you're someone's friend you're always someone's friend.

One of the things I see in our society that bothers me is how so many people are like Orpah, they are only a "friend" if there is something in it for them. As long as they can get something out of this friendship then they will be your friend. This is nothing more than being an opportunist. A true friend will be there for you when you have nothing to offer them. Yes, maybe at one time in this friendship you benefited from making someone your friend, but your friendship with a person is revealed when they have nothing to offer and you actually seem to lose by calling them your friend. You should never be the type of person who forsakes your friend when everyone else forsakes them.

Listen, if you can't be a friend when a person is in the greatest need of friendship, then you are not a real friend. Just because a person has done something very wrong in their life does not mean you should forsake them. Sometimes being a friend to someone takes character, and this is lacking in our society. Just because a person has attacked you out of hurt does not mean that your friendship with them should end. A true friend will be there for a person through thick and thin.

What type of friend are you? Are you like Orpah who will only be a good friend when people have something to offer you? Or, are you like Ruth who will stay true as a friend even when they have lost everything in life and have nothing which you can benefit from out of this friendship? Christians ought to be known as people who are true friends. One thing you should strive for in your life is to be known as a person who is a friend to people when they are at the lowest part of their lives. Let's be careful about becoming friends just because we benefit from that relationship. Let's be a people who are true to our friends during their lowest moments of life.

Are You Listening?

1 Samuel 3:9

"Therefore Eli said unto Samuel, Go, lie down: and it shall be, if he call thee, that thou shalt say, Speak, LORD; for thy servant heareth. So Samuel went and lay down in his place."

According to the Bible, Samuel was a young man who had grown up in the temple. We find in previous chapters that he was Hannah's answer to prayer. Because he was an answer to prayer, Hannah promised to give God the child so he could grow up in the temple. After many years of Samuel growing up in the temple, the LORD came to him at night and called him. Samuel, not knowing the voice of the LORD, ran to Eli the priest and asked him what he wanted. Eli, not calling Samuel, told him to go back to bed. This happened two more times before Eli realized that the LORD was trying to speak to Samuel. Eli then told Samuel that the next time he heard this voice he was to say, *"...Speak, LORD; for thy servant heareth..."*

I fear in our lives that God tries to speak to us, but we are so busy with our schedules that we can't hear His voice. No, I am not talking about God speaking in an audible voice; I am talking about God speaking to us through the avenues of life through which He normally speaks to His people today.

For instance, are you listening to God as He tries to speak to you through His Word, the Bible? Every morning God would love to speak to your heart through the reading of the Word of God. Our problem is we want to sleep in and get a few extra minutes of rest when the voice of God could speak to us, but we are asleep.

Are you listening when God tries to speak to you through the avenue of prayer? I find many times in my life that God speaks to me when I am praying. It is amazing that as I am asking God what to do about a situation in prayer that God gives me the answer as I pray to Him. Are you not hearing God's voice because you are not praying?

I ask you again, are you listening to the voice of God through preaching? Too many times people come to church and could hear the voice of God speak to their hearts during the preaching time, but because they only come to fulfill their religious obligation for the week, they don't hear God's voice. God will speak to you in the preaching time if you will only listen. By the way, God can't speak to you through preaching if you are not in church when you are supposed to be. It's not that God's voice is not speaking to you; it is that you are not listening to God.

I ask you one more time, are you listening to God through the circumstances of life. Many times God tries to speak to His people through life's circumstances, but because we don't stop to listen, we cannot hear His voice. In every circumstance of life, we should stop and listen to what God is trying to teach us through that circumstance. Listen to what God is trying to teach you through your circumstances.

Be careful not to let the noise of life's schedule get so loud that you can't hear the voice of God in your life. Every day of your life you should wake up with the prayer to God, "...Speak, LORD, for thy servant heareth."

Whose Side are You On?

1 Samuel 10:26-27

"And Saul also went home to Gibeah; and there went with him a band of men, whose hearts God had touched. But the children of Belial said, How shall this man save us? And they despised him, and brought him no presents. But he held his peace."

The story in this chapter is about the anointing of Saul as king over Israel. Samuel, the prophet, called all the people together to show them who their king was going to be. As Samuel began to separate the tribes and families to narrow down the search for the new king, Saul's family was taken and Saul was chosen by God to become the new king of Israel.

What is interesting to me is that as Saul was chosen, the Bible states there went with Saul *"...a band of men, whose hearts God had touched."* But then we read in the very next verse that there were also some men who were critical of the new king. What caused them to be so critical? Though the Bible does not state, I believe the reason was jealousy. I think they were jealous that Saul was chosen and they weren't. This is why they despised him in their hearts because they wanted the position that Saul was going to hold. What we must see though, is that I would rather have been on the side of the men who followed Saul than the men who would not follow him, because, we find later that Saul was the right choice, and God did work through this young man.

Recently, I helped a couple of pastors who lost several people in their churches. In both cases, the reason why they lost people is because a disloyal person had questioned the man of God's decisions and how he was leading the church. What is interesting in both of these cases is that the decisions the men of God were making had nothing to do with doctrine, they only had to deal with a direction in which they thought their church should go. In both of these cases it was a sharp individual, who wanted position, which caused the problems in these churches. How sad that these men who have so much potential would fall on the wrong side of the man of God and lead others astray with them.

Let me be very blunt with you, when it comes to choosing whose side you should fall on in a situation at your church, you would always be wise to fall on the side of the man of God. Very rarely have I ever seen people choose the other side and be right. Now as sure as I say this I know there will be someone who is the exception to the rule, but the majority of the time the man of God is right. Unless the preacher is starting to lead the church in a different direction doctrinally, you would be better off following the man of God. I know you may not always understand everything about a situation in your church, but it is always safer to be on the man of God's side than it is to be on the side of the person who stands against the man of God.

Notice what God called these men who stood against Saul, He called them *"...children of Belial..."* I say all of this for one purpose, I want you to be blessed in your life. I have found in my own life that I am safer backing the man of God than I am standing against the man of God. I would rather be wrong about standing with the man of God than be wrong about standing against the man of God. I have never seen God punish people for standing with the man of God, but all through the Bible you see how God punished people who stood against the man of God. Other than compromise and doctrinal error, always choose the side that the man of God stands on; this is always the safest choice.

God Remembers

1 Samuel 15:2

"Thus saith the LORD of hosts, I remember that which Amalek did to Israel, how he laid wait for him in the way, when he came up from Egypt."

Have you ever wondered if God is going to come through on His Word and punish those who have attacked His people? At times in the Christian life we almost lose hope that those who do us wrong will ever pay for their wrong doing.

God came to Samuel and told him to have Israel go and utterly destroy the Amalekites for what they did to Israel when they were coming up from Egypt into the Promised Land. The statement in this verse that should encourage all of God's people is, *"Thus saith the LORD of hosts, I remember..."* How thankful these people should have been that God had a memory that would remember those who tried to hurt them. Every Christian should take solace in this statement because God does remember and He remembers many things.

He remembers what the heathen do unto the people of God. I know it seems that the heathen get away with their wickedness, but let me assure you, God remembers. He remembers how they have gossiped and attacked you. He remembers the very acts and what the heathen have done against the church of God. Don't despair Christian, God remembers!

He remembers what people do to Him as well. God remembers what the judges and politicians do to try and kick Him out of society. He remembers how Hollywood and their wicked society have blasphemed His name and integrity. He remembers the actions of individuals who make it their plot in life to be sure that God's name is removed from every public meeting place. Yes, God remembers!

Let me also encourage you that God remembers the good that Christians do as well. Though at times you wonder if God even sees what you are doing; let me assure you that God not only sees, but He will remember all that you have done for Him. God will remember the work you do every weekend in your ministry. God will remember the sacrifice you made to give money to those when you had no money yourself. God will remember how you went without to make sure the missionary support you promised was paid. Christian, don't despair, God remembers!

Though days, months and years pass by and you see no action on God's behalf, let me assure you that God remembers. You may think that God has forgotten all that you have done, but you can take this verse to heart; God remembers. God is not a forgetful God; God is a God whose memory will never be lost. You can take encouragement today in this statement that God remembers, and when He remembers, He will pay back that which you have suffered and given for His cause.

Life's Unpleasantries

1 Samuel 18:9
"And Saul eyed David from that day and forward."

Did you ever have a time when you were a child that you stood waiting to be picked for a team and you were one of the last ones chosen to be on the team? It may have been for a game or some task, but whatever it was, you felt like you were the fifth-wheel on the team. They always seemed to give you the position or the job that nobody else wanted.

Life can be that way at times when the lot that you are handed is unpleasant. But, it is how you handle this lot in life that determines your ultimate outcome. When I look at the life of Saul, he was handed a most unpleasant thing when he was told that the kingdom would be taken from him and handed to another. As we read about Saul, we see in this chapter he perceived that David was the one who was going to get the kingdom. What I want you to notice is the response Saul had towards this unpleasantry. His response was jealousy and anger.

Yet, when I think of how Saul responded, I think of another person who was handed the very same judgment from God, and that person was Moses. The difference between Moses and Saul was Moses accepted his lot and moved on and made the best out of it. Both men had done wrong which caused them their lot, but their handling of the situation is what led to the different endings of their lives. Moses, because he handled his situation right, was buried by God and considered a hero. Saul, because he handled his situation wrong, lived the rest of his life in bitterness, jealousy and anger and died without being desired.

Many times we feel that we are a fifth-wheel in life when we are handed the most unpleasant lot in life. It is how we handle this situation that determines how our life will end up. Whether you are the one who caused your situation or whether God just decided to give you that situation is not the issue, it is how you handle it once it has been handed to you that is the issue. When you take the unpleasantries of life and decide to make the best out of them, you can see that your life will be used in a great way just as we see in the life of Moses. But, when you let the unpleasantries of life get to you, your life will be filled with jealousy, bitterness, anger and unhappiness.

I don't know what life has dealt you, but to many who read these devotionals, life most certainly has given you an unpleasant lot to deal with. It is what you determine to do with your unpleasant lot which will ultimately determine what the quality of the rest of your life will be. What you need to do is take that unpleasantry and decide to use it to help others. Instead of letting it make you an unpleasant person, let it be the tool you use to be useful for the rest of your life. It is how you choose to face life's unpleasant lots that will determine how you will be seen in the eyes of others.

Always remember, when life deals you an unpleasant lot, and you seem to get the bad end of the stick, take whatever you have been handed and be like Moses and make the best out of what you have been dealt. Take the lemon that you have been handed in your life and make lemonade!

Thanks for Nothing!

1 Samuel 23:12

"Then said David, Will the men of Keilah deliver me and my men into the hand of Saul? And the LORD said, They will deliver thee up."

I find the story in this verse to be an amazing story. David and his men just finished defending the city of Keilah from captivity and destruction. The Philistines tried to invade this little city, but David and his men defended the city from the Philistine's attack. After the attack, you would think that David and his men would be safe from Saul's evil desire to kill him. But when David heard that Saul was coming to the city, he asked God if the men of the city would deliver him into the hands of Saul. God told David that they would and that he should leave the city.

What a way to say, "Thank you" to someone who just saved your life. Just think, David had just saved the lives of many of these men. David had just saved the lives of many of the ladies of this town. David had saved many of the children of this city from bondage to the Philistines. Their way of saying, "Thank you" was to turn him over to Saul who wanted to kill him. Thanks for nothing!

Gratitude seems to be something of the past anymore. Too many times, as I travel, I see those who give everything they have to help people and then those same people turn on them. Let me point out a couple of things about this thought.

First of all, don't be guilty of being like the people of Keilah who showed their gratitude to the one who helped them by turning on him. As a church member, don't be guilty of showing your gratitude to your pastor by turning on him after he has helped you through his counseling and preaching. As a child, don't show your gratitude to your parents by turning on them and breaking their hearts by living a wicked lifestyle. As an individual, be careful about turning on those who have invested in your life. We may not always get along with people, but what a horrible way to say thank you by trying to hurt the very one who has helped us tremendously in our lives.

Secondly, if someone has turned on you after you have helped them greatly, don't let that stop you from helping others. Yes, you will be used in life, but you must remember that the reason we are in the ministry is to be used by people. There are people whose lives would be a wreck without your help. For them to turn on you can hurt very deeply. Don't let that hurt stop you from helping people. That is exactly what the Devil would want for you to do. Just because people have hurt us does not mean that we should stop helping others.

Watch yourself and your spirit so that you don't let these hurts destroy your helpful spirit. Let's all work at being a people who show gratitude to those who have helped us in our lives. No one should be able to say about us, "Thanks for nothing!"

Turning Friends Into Enemies

1 Samuel 27:4

"And it was told Saul that David was fled to Gath: and he sought no more again for him."

I hate to say this, but many times the enemies that we have in life are enemies created because of our own actions. Though this is not the case all of the time, there is something that caused that relationship to go awry.

The story between Saul and David is a sad story in the fact that here are two men who, if they would have worked together, could have accomplished a lot for the nation of Israel. These men were not only on the same side as God, but they were also relatives in that David married the daughter of Saul. Yet when we come to this verse, we see David fled to the Philistines to save his own life. The Philistines were the enemies of the Israelites. Now David is on the opposite side of Saul because of grave mistakes that Saul made. Let me show you a few of the mistakes that Saul made which turned a promising friendship into bitter enemies. If we make these same mistakes they will cause us to develop enemies of our own making.

First of all, Saul lied to David and this started the road to them becoming enemies. Nothing will turn a relationship bad quicker than people lying to each other. When spouses lie to each other, it will start destroying that relationship. When friends lie to each other, it will hurt their good relationship. Telling the truth may be hard at times, but telling the truth won't turn good friends into bitter enemies.

Secondly, Saul was very hard on David. What I mean by this is Saul expected more out of David than he did anyone else. When you treat one person differently than you would treat someone else, you are headed down the road of turning that someone into your enemy. Be careful that you treat everyone the same.

Thirdly, Saul became jealous of the blessings of God on David's life. Jealousy will destroy any relationship. You must be careful that you aren't jealous of someone because of the good happening in their life. This is caused by pure selfishness which is nothing more than a heart problem of our own. Rejoice when good happens to people, and work harder so that it can happen to you.

Fourth, Saul became deceitful in his dealings with David. If you want to avoid making someone your enemy, then don't be deceitful in your dealings with them. Saul, in order to kill David, had David go and battle the Philistines by himself. This was deceitful at best, evil at worst. In order to keep yourself from turning friends into enemies, always be upright in your dealings with people. Don't do underhanded or shady dealings with people; this will lead to hard feelings down the road.

Last of all, Saul made everything about himself. This will turn people off more than you could ever imagine. Life is not all about you. For any relationship to work, both sides must be givers. If you really want it to work, then give to the relationship without expecting anything in return.

No one likes enemies! If you start accomplishing things in life you will have your enemies; you can't avoid that. But we can avoid actions which will make enemies out of our friends. Let's avoid the actions of Saul so as to avoid making our friends our bitter enemies.

Respect the Power

2 Samuel 6:9

"And David was afraid of the LORD that day, and said, How shall the ark of the LORD come to me?"

Years ago I used to work in construction for a custom builder. We built houses from the foundation to the last touch-up in the house. There were also times when we would remodel houses. I remember one time in particular that we were remodeling a house when my boss told me to start tearing out the electrical wiring in one section of the home. He assured me the circuit breakers had been kicked off and that I would be safe pulling the wires. I remember grabbing one wire and getting the shock of my life. The breaker for that wire apparently had not been shut off! What a valuable lesson this little wire gave me for the rest of my life. The lesson; always respect the power. The power that flows through that wire can either help me or hurt me; it all depends on if I am using it the right way or not.

David unfortunately learned the same lesson with God. David wanted to move the Ark of the Covenant to the city in which he lived because he wanted the blessings of God on his life. In the process of moving the Ark, he chose a wrong way to move it which resulted in the death of a young man. This verse shows us that it was this very action that caused David to get the proper respect for the LORD and His power.

Every Christian should learn a lesson from David and that is the power of God, if used properly, will help us tremendously; if used in a wrong manner it can hurt us. God's power is far greater that we can handle. God's power is not there to hurt us; it is there to help us. If we do wrong in our lives or use the wrong methods of serving God, we will experience God's power in an adverse manner. If we serve God and do right, then God's power will be an asset to our lives and ministries. God's power in this case will help us accomplish more than what we normally could under our own strength and power.

Each of us needs to learn to respect the power of God. We should never take God's power for granted; the very moment that we take that power for granted is the very moment we will end up hurting ourselves. Never forget that God has the power to help or hurt us. If we keep this in mind in our daily lives, I believe we will find ourselves doing right knowing that God's power is there for our benefit. God's power can also hurt us if we take the wrong steps in life. Let's learn to keep in mind that God's power is greater than we can handle. Because of this we must always respect the power of God. When we respect His power it will help us instead of hurting us.

She Came In

2 Samuel 11:4

"And David sent messengers, and took her; and she came in unto him, and he lay with her; for she was purified from her uncleanness: and she returned unto her house."

In the story of David and Bathsheba, I believe there is something missed by most people. Most of the time David gets the blame, and he should receive part of the blame for what happened between him and Bathsheba. He was wrong in his actions of committing adultery with Bathsheba, and he rightfully gets the blame for what happened; but, Bathsheba was just as much to blame for what happened as David was.

You can't read this story with blinders on blaming David for what happened, for if you do you will miss some of the truths that will teach us how to live pure lives. When you read this story, you see there were some things Bathsheba did that contributed to this act of adultery. First, she was indecent. Though David should not have looked at her when she was indecent, she should have made sure that no one could see her. There is something called curtains, and they had them in those days. Secondly, you will notice that when David called for her, the Bible says, *"...she came in unto him..."* If she had never come, David would have never had the opportunity to do wrong with her. Bathsheba was just as much at fault in this adulterous affair as David was, don't forget that.

In all immoral relationships, there are always two people who are to blame. We live in a society that wants to blame the male for all the wrong for this is politically correct, but it always takes two for an immoral relationship to occur. Of course, I am not blaming a woman when a man may force her, but what I'm talking about is when two do wrong

TOGETHER. I believe some of this can be avoided if ladies learn to be proper in a couple of areas. Ladies, learn to be decent all of the time. I am not just talking about in private matters; I am also talking about in your dress. In our society, ladies want to be provocative with their dress, and then we wonder why we are in the shape we are in. Ladies, be careful to wear clothing that doesn't reveal yourself causing men to lust after you. Though men should have the character to turn their heads and say, "No," ladies are just as guilty when they wear clothing that invites a man. If you don't want to invite men, then don't dress like you are inviting them. Ladies can still dress sharp, and yet not dress in such a provocative way.

Secondly, ladies, you can always say, "No!" to the advances of men. Though a man should never make an advance on a lady who is married, a lady has the power to stop the advances very quickly. Ladies must be careful not to be flirtatious with their actions towards men. Ladies should be careful to act properly around men. If a man starts making advances towards a married lady, then the married lady should immediately stop any more advances by letting him know that she is not available because she is married.

Though much more could be said about this subject, all I want to warn people about is stopping things before they get to the point when wrong occurs. It is always better to stop any wrong at the first sign of it, than waiting until emotions are involved and it is then too hard to say, "No."

To those who are married, realize you made a vow to your spouse and you should be a person of your word. If we don't want to end up where David and Bathsheba ended up, then both sides need to be proper in their actions towards the opposite gender.

David's Friend

2 Samuel 15:37

"So Hushai David's friend came into the city, and Absalom came into Jerusalem."

One of the blessings of David's battle with his son Absalom was that he found out who his friends really were. When David fled for his life because of the disloyalty of Absalom, there were many people who called themselves friends to David who stayed and served Absalom. Ahithophel was one of those. But one friend that David had was Hushai, for he, in the midst of the treason, stood with David even to the point of putting his life in danger. He was a friend in the truest sense.

The test of friendship is adversity. You will find out who your friends are when adversity comes into your life. Without adversity you will never know who your friends are. It is always easy to call someone your friend when they are on the top in their life. When adversity comes and everyone stands against them, the test of whether you are a friend is if you are willing to stand with them during their difficult time.

I am afraid that most people are fair-weather friends. As long as times are good they will stand with you, but at the first sign of adversity they leave you. Though we may think that adverse times in our life are a curse, in one sense it is a blessing for it is during these times we find out who our friends really are. If you want to find out who your friends are, check and see who visits you when you are in the hospital. Look who calls you up and prays with you when others stand against you. Look around and see who is willing to risk their name just to be called your friend. Those who will do these things are your true friends.

Christian, we should be a friend to others. One of the traits of the world is that they only stand with you when it benefits them. We ought not to carry this trait. Instead, we should be like Christ Who promises to be *"...a friend that sticketh closer than a brother."* (Proverbs 18:24) We should never be a people who only stand with the pastor when times are good. We should be a people who stand with the pastor when times are bad. We should be a people, who when adverse times come for those around us, we are willing to stand with them even if it means others will forsake us. When someone messes up their life in sin, we should be a people who are there for them when everyone else has left them. This is a true friend!

Let me ask you; are you a friend to those with whom you are acquainted? Are you the type of person, who when adversity comes in the lives of others, you stand beside them? This should be one of the things for which you are known. Whatever you accomplish in life, make one of your accomplishments to be a friend to others. When I say friend, I mean a friend in the truest sense; standing with one during their time of adversity.

Overreacting

2 Samuel 20:19

"I am one of them that are peaceable and faithful in Israel: thou seekest to destroy a city and a mother in Israel: why wilt thou swallow up the inheritance of the LORD?"

Several years ago my wife and I were at a church together when all of a sudden we heard a woman screaming outside. No one knew what was going on, so as people normally would do, we ran outside to see what happened. As we arrived where the woman was, we saw her holding a can of spray paint screaming because her child had somehow got some paint in his eyes. I watched with amazement as the husband was trying to calm her down so he could take care of the child. Overreacting is no doubt the key word in this story. Her overreaction to the situation was not helping anybody; it was only making the situation worse.

This story about Joab pursuing after Sheba is a classic example of overreacting to a situation. Yes, Sheba needed to be dealt with, but to try and destroy a whole city for one person was a definite overreaction. If it wasn't for a wise woman in the city, who encouraged all sides to think more rationally, a whole city would have been destroyed.

Each of us must be careful not to overreact to the situations we face in life. Parents must be careful to not overreact to our children's actions and problems. School personnel must be careful about overreacting to the situations that happen in the school. Church staff and workers must be careful about overreaction. Employers and government workers all must be careful that they don't let overreaction cause their problems to get worse.

One of the main reasons for overreaction is lack of training. We can't always know what kind of training we need in life, for we don't always know what situations we are going to face. Therefore when situations arise that must be dealt with immediately, we must learn to be careful not to overreact. The best way to keep yourself from overreacting is simply to stop and think before you act. Instead of acting without thinking, which is overreacting, you need to stop and survey the situation so that you can come up with a rational reaction.

The next time you are faced with a situation that must be dealt with immediately, be careful that you don't overreact. Always remember before you act, you must stop and think so that your reaction doesn't make the situation worse.

Source of Strife

Proverbs 22:10

"Cast out the scorner, and contention shall go out; yea, strife and reproach shall cease."

Strife and contention are an unpleasant part of life that we all must endure. Unfortunately, because we have humans who are involved in the work of the LORD, you will find contention and strife among those who are doing God's work.

The Bible shows us that the source of strife and contention is the scorner. It is always the scorner who causes the strife. It is always the scorner who causes contention in relationships. This is why God said that if you want to stop the strife and contention then you must get rid of the scorner.

If the scorner is the problem, then we should know how to identify the scorner. The scorner is one who ridicules truth. The scorner is one who makes fun of sin. For instance, a scorner is one who will look at the truths of the Word of God and try to change those truths to fit today's politically correct society. A scorner is one who ignores what the Bible plainly teaches and will teach what they want for their own personal advancement. A scorner is one who teaches that God's Word is not true and makes a mockery of those who believe in God's Word. A scorner is also being one who laughs at sin and thinks it is funny.

I have said all of this to help us understand why many times we seem to have strife and contention in our homes and lives. When we watch Hollywood programs and movies that scoff at truth and laugh at wrong, then this is why we end up with a life filled with strife and contention. Not always will it be contention and strife with others, it many times is an inward strife and contention which we face. This is why you see many Christians who are unhappy. They have a life filled with contention and strife caused by the scorner's influence in their lives.

If we want peace in our lives, then we need to look at who and what we allow to influence our lives and see if scorners are having a part of that influence. If they are, then we must cast out that which scorns at the truth and purity of the Word of God. We all can have peace in life if we will get rid of the source of contention and strife; that source is the scorners whom we allow to influence us. Let's be a people who cast out the scorners and only allow those who love truth and hate sin to influence our life.

Setting Yourself Apart From the Rest

1 Kings 9:4

"And if thou wilt walk before me, as David thy father walked, in integrity of heart, and in uprightness, to do according to all that I have commanded thee, and wilt keep my statutes and my judgments:"

King David was no doubt a man who had set himself apart from the rest of the crowd. When you study the kings of Israel you will see that they are always compared to King David. I believe the reason for this is that David set himself apart from the rest of the crowd with his actions.

You may ask, what are these actions that set him apart from the rest? We find in this verse these actions. They included the way he conducted himself with people and with God and the source from where those actions came. That source was his heart. It was David having a heart of integrity and uprightness to do God's commandments which set him apart from the rest of the kings of Israel. David had a sincere desire in his heart to do right. He always wanted to make sure he pleased God. But even greater than that, he walked honestly and tried to do the right thing all of the time. This is what set him apart from the rest. God told Solomon that he could have the same blessings as his father if he would do what David did in his life.

God is a God Who is just with all people. In other words, if God does something for one, He will do the same thing for everyone else. If this be the case, then if we want to have an established life as verse 5 says, then we must do what David did to set himself apart from the rest. His actions set him apart from the rest, and that established the life and kingdom of David.

If you want to be established then you must obtain a sincere desire to do right within your heart. What I mean by this is that in your heart you must have a burning desire to do right all of the time. In everything you do you must want to do the right thing. It must be the desire of your heart to please God with all of your actions. Oh, you may do wrong at times as David certainly did, but your heart must be a heart that desires to do right.

Then, if we want to be established, we must live our lives walking honestly among people. In other words we must always try to do the right thing with people. The desire of our life should be to make sure all of our dealings with people are not self-serving, thus always doing what is right by other people.

You will notice, both of these things are about doing right; but one is doing right with God and the other is doing right with man. God says this is what will establish a person in their life. This is what sets a person apart from everyone else when they do right with God and when they also do right with man.

Are you one of many or are you a person who has been set apart from everyone else because of your desire to do right with both God and man? When you live your life and make it your heart's desire to do right with God and man, this type of living will set you apart from everyone else and will stabilize and establish your life.

Stop Fooling Yourself

1 Kings 14:2

"And Jeroboam said to his wife, Arise, I pray thee, and disguise thyself, that thou be not known to be the wife of Jeroboam; and get thee to Shiloh: behold, there is Ahijah the prophet, which told me that I should be king over this people."

I find in this story a mistake that many people make in their relationship with God. Too many times we think we can fool God, but the only one who we are truthfully fooling is ourselves.

Jeroboam told his wife to go find the Prophet Ahijah and find out if their son would recover from his sickness. He told his wife to disguise herself so the man of God would not know who she was because he felt that Ahijah had a grudge against him. The problem with disguising herself with the man of God is that she did not take into consideration the God Who this man represented. Because she did not take this into consideration, the only one who she was really fooling was herself.

Many people live a life of deception trying to make an impression upon man when the One Who they should try to make the impression upon is God. We cannot fool God no matter how good we are at fooling people. God knows our hearts and He also knows all the details of our private lives. Because God knows our hearts, the only one who we are fooling with our disguise of Christianity is ourselves.

Listen, you are only fooling yourself if you have never accepted Christ as your Saviour. Do you think you are going to sneak your way into Heaven by fooling God when you know in your heart you are not saved? It does not matter if everyone else thinks you are saved; stop fooling yourself and get saved, for you will not fool God.

Do you think you can fool God with a facade of Christianity when God knows the very thoughts and intents of your heart? Don't you understand that even if you are able to fool everyone else with your actions, your heart is revealed to God? The only one who you are fooling is yourself. Eventually God will judge you for your thoughts and the sins which you perform in private. Instead of living a disguise, what we ought to do is get right with God. This is the action that impresses God the most, and this is the action that will bring the blessings of God upon our lives.

Have you been fooling yourself lately with the life you are living? Always remember, you may fool man with your disguise, but you will never fool God. Let's live with the realization that our private lives are what we must keep right. If our private lives are right then our public lives will take care of themselves.

Do Your Job

1 Kings 12:26
"And Jeroboam said in his heart, Now shall the kingdom return to the house of David:"

When you read this story you must keep in mind the background of Jeroboam as he just became the king of Israel. He served under Solomon and, according to the Bible, Jeroboam was a very industrious man. Because of his hard work he was promoted in Solomon's kingdom until Solomon felt that Jeroboam was a threat to his leadership. Jeroboam fled and did not come back to Israel until Rehoboam became king.

Rehoboam made a foolish decision which caused the kingdom to be divided. In the division ten tribes followed Jeroboam and made him their king. Now that Jeroboam was their king he made a classic mistake that many leaders make; he was afraid of losing his position and title. Because of this fear, he set up two golden calves and had the people worship those calves. This action brought God's judgment upon the house of Jeroboam.

As a leader, you cannot lead properly when you lead with fear of losing your position. Leaders do not lead because they want to lead, leaders lead because there is a need for them to lead. Great leaders do not lead with the fear of losing their position; they lead by just doing their job. By doing their job they will become great leaders.

If you are a leader in some realm, whether it is in your community, church, organization or home, you must never lead to keep your position. If you do this, you will hurt those who follow you, and you will do whatever it takes to keep your position including compromise. When your position becomes more important to you as a leader than doing your job then you have set yourself up to compromise. Though there are many other areas that can cause a leader to compromise, we must be careful to just do our job. It was our actions of doing our job that gave us the position of leadership in the first place, so it will be us continuing to do what we have always done that will help us to keep our position of leadership.

Leaders, don't get so enamored with your position that you will do whatever it takes to keep that position. This will lead to sin and compromise. Instead, your leadership should simply be you doing your job. By doing your job you will secure your position of leadership.

License to Sin

1 Kings 21:7

"And Jezebel his wife said unto him, Dost thou now govern the kingdom of Israel? arise, and eat bread, and let thine heart be merry: I will give thee the vineyard of Naboth the Jezreelite."

One of the mistakes those who hold position commonly make is they think their position gives them a right to do whatever they want to do. Many times those in position think they are not accountable to anyone, and this is not true.

Ahab went to Naboth to ask if he could buy his vineyard from him. There was nothing wrong with this. When Naboth said he would not sell his vineyard, Ahab went home and pouted to his wife Jezebel. Jezebel reminded Ahab that he was the King of Israel as if his position gave him a right to do anything he wanted to do. This is where Ahab and Jezebel went wrong; position never gives you a license to do wrong. Sin is sin no matter who does it and no matter what position that person may hold. Just because you hold a position does not give you a license to sin.

Parent, be careful about thinking as a parent you can do what you tell your children not to do. If it is wrong for your children to lie, then it is wrong for you to lie. Don't live a double-standard! If it is wrong for your children to cheat on their schoolwork, then it is wrong for you to cheat on your taxes or finances. Whatever is wrong for your children is wrong for you too.

A policeman is not above the law either. If it is wrong for a person being questioned by the police to lie about their actions, then it is wrong for the police to lie to the one being questioned. If it is wrong for the driver of a car to speed then it is wrong for the policeman to speed as well. Position NEVER gives a person the right to do wrong. If it is wrong for a citizen to disobey the laws of the land, then it is wrong for the President and all lawmakers to disobey the law. Position never gives anyone the right to do wrong.

Be careful about thinking your position gives you the right to do wrong. God holds both the one who has position and the one who follows to the same level of accountability. Be careful about living a double-standard; if you expect others to do something, then you had better do what you expect them to do. Position never gives you a license to sin and do wrong!

Dig the Ditches

2 Kings 3:16
"And he said, Thus saith the LORD, Make this valley full of ditches."

Israel had once again been invaded by the Midianites. The army of the Midianites seemed to be an army that was too big for Israel to overcome. But, anytime you have God on your side it matters not what the size of the obstacle is that is in front of you. As long as God is with you, you will win in spite of the situation you face.

Elisha came to the king of Israel to deliver a message to him that God was going to deliver them from this great army who had come to destroy them. There was only one stipulation that God's people must perform in order for God to perform this great miracle for them; go and dig some ditches for God to fill. God said he would fill these ditches with water if they would only dig the ditches.

I find in many cases the reason people do not see miracles in their lives is not because God does not want to perform miracles for them, it's that God's people will not do the work necessary for God to do the miracle. You will notice in this story that the miracle was theirs on the condition that they would dig the ditches.

In churches and in the lives of Christians, the miracles of God are ours if we will only dig the ditches. God wants to do a miracle in your church and help grow your church, but someone must dig the ditches in order for God to fill those ditches. I am talking about the bus routes and Sunday school classes that God would love to do a work through, but He can only fill the busses and the Sunday school classes if people will go out and work to fill those busses and classes.

Notice, they had to dig the ditches. I don't know if you have ever dug a ditch, but it takes work to dig ditches, and it takes work for God to bless our ministries. This is why we call it the **work** of the LORD. God is not going to bless a life or ministry where work is not being done. You can complain all you want about your church not growing, but what are you doing to help grow the church? Someone must dig the ditches in your church in order for your church to grow.

I ask you, what ditches are you digging to help build your church? Let me put it very plainly, in what ministries do you work? I did not ask what ministry you participate in, but in what ministry do you work? God wants to bless our churches, but it takes people like you to work in our churches for God to bless as He desires.

I say to those who read this, find a "shovel" which is nothing more than a ministry and start digging or working in a ministry so God can bless that ministry with miracles. It takes people willing to work for God to perform miracles. Don't you be guilty of holding back God's miracles because of your lack of work.

The Power of Influence

2 Kings 15:28

"And he did that which was evil in the sight of the LORD: he departed not from the sins of Jeroboam the son of Nebat, who made Israel to sin."

One thing that catches my attention all throughout this book is the influence one person had on the many generations that followed. For instance, Ahab influenced many generations that followed him for bad. David influenced many generations that followed him for good. The influence of one life upon several hundred and even thousands of lives that follow them is very astounding.

We can see in this verse that Jeroboam was one of those people who influenced several generations after he was gone. Notice the Bible says in this verse that Azariah did evil and *"...departed not from the sins of Jeroboam..."* Three to four generations after Jeroboam was dead his sins still influenced people. I seriously doubt that he understood the heartache that the actions of his life would cause to the several generations who followed him. If he would have understood this, I believe he may have changed his lifestyle, for very few people want to influence future generations for wrong.

With this in mind, we must be very careful how we live our lives. We never know who we are influencing and how long the results of our actions will go on after we are gone. The power of our influence is greater than what we really realize. We must keep in mind that every decision we make may influence several generations to come.

Parent, be careful with your actions. You never know how you will affect your family for generations to come with your actions. Preacher, be very careful with the decisions you make concerning the direction that you choose to serve God. You must realize that as a preacher the direction you choose will affect several generations to come and will touch every person's life that you influence. Every leader in the church, whether you are a Sunday school teacher or ministry leader, you must be careful for your life will influence generations to come.

How careful we must be to keep this in the forefront of our minds as we walk throughout the day. Remember, if you yield when you are tempted to do wrong you will influence generations to come. I don't think you want this hanging over your head the rest of your life. Remember, when you are trying to decide to do right, that your decision to do right could influence generations to come to also do right. Let's always remember the power of influence does not only influence those whom we are currently over, but the power of influence will affect future generations as well. Let's be very careful with our actions!

Plugged Ears and Hardened Necks

2 Kings 17:14

"Notwithstanding they would not hear, but hardened their necks, like to the neck of their fathers, that did not believe in the LORD their God."

What a sad commentary of these people in this verse when God said, *"...they would not hear, but hardened their necks..."* Here are a people for whom God had done great things. Here are a people also had seen the presence of God. Here are a people who had heard the voice of God. Here are a people whom God chose to be His people.

Now, after several hundred years, they forgot their history and the great works that God did among them. In an attempt to bring these people back to Him, He sent preachers to preach His Word; and yet they would not come back. He sent pestilence their way; and yet they would not come back. He sent wars their way to bring them back, yet they would not come back. He sent hard times and sickness their way, yet they would not come back. In fact, they seemed to be a people who had plugged their ears to the voice of God and hardened their necks to the commands of God. What a shame!

When I look at America and what God has done for her, in amazement I see a nation who has plugged her ears to God's voice and hardened her neck to His commands. After all the grace God has bestowed upon America, we continually seem to be a nation who thumbs its nose at God and tells God to leave us alone. You see the same commentary in the lives of many Christians; people whom God has blessed far beyond what they deserve, people whom God has saved from their sins, people whom God has blessed financially and with many material blessings, and yet, they still plug their ears at the voice of God and harden their necks at His commands.

My warning to America and every Christian who reads this devotional is: God will not put up with our foolishness forever. You may be getting away with plugging your ears to His voice now, but one day you will receive the rewards of your wicked acts. You may continue to harden your neck to God's command and refuse to do what He tells you to do and only do what you want to do, but you will receive the reward for your actions.

Let's be careful about being a people who plug their ears at the voice of God and instead let's listen to His voice. When I say listen, I mean do what He tells us to do. This is where true blessings lie and this is where true happiness in life can be found; in the center of God's will.

Getting the Ear of God

2 Kings 22:19

"Because thine heart was tender, and thou hast humbled thyself before the LORD, when thou heardest what I spake against this place, and against the inhabitants thereof, that they should become a desolation and a curse, and hast rent thy clothes, and wept before me; I also have heard thee, saith the LORD."

This chapter tells the story of Josiah becoming king of Judah. When he was old enough to start making decisions for himself, one of the first actions he performed was to have the priests clean the house of the LORD. As they cleaned the house of the LORD, the priests found the Word of God buried in the rubbish of the temple. They gave the Word of God to Shaphan, who read It to King Josiah. As the Word of God was read, the Bible states that Josiah realized the dire condition that God's people were in, rent his clothes and prayed, asking God to show mercy upon His people.

In the verse above, there were four things that caused Josiah to get the ear of God. The privilege of having God's ear brought mercy and revival from God to His people. What were these four things that caused him to have the ear of God? First, his tender heart got the ear of God. Then, we see humbling himself before God allowed him to get God's ear. Then, immediately responding to God's voice caused God to want to give His ear to Josiah. Lastly, his weeping out of a need for God to do something grabbed God's attention. These four things allowed Josiah to get the ear of God.

I don't know a Christian who would not want to have the ear of God. Every Christian would love to have God's ear when they pray. The reason we don't have His ear is because we don't have the four characteristics Josiah had which caused him to get God's ear. Would you like to have the confidence of knowing you have the ear of God? Do you desire the type of confidence where, when you pray, you know He hears your prayer? If you would like to have God's ear, you better check to see if you have a tender heart towards God. Have a heart that is soft and pliable in which God can work? One thing that will get God's attention is a heart that is tender towards Him.

You must also be a person who practices humility, being modest of your own worth without any ounce of arrogance in your heart will most certainly get the ear of God. God wants to hear the prayer of those who realize they are nothing without Him.

If you want to have the ear of God, be a person who responds to His voice when He speaks. Why should God give you His ear when you won't respond when He does speak? The problem is not that God won't hear and answer; it's that we won't hear and do. Our response to God's voice weighs heavily on whether God will give us His ear.

Last of all, if you want the ear of God, there must be times when you simply cry out to Him. I am talking about a literal weeping with a broken heart where you must have God or you are going to die. This type of prayer gets God's attention. Throughout the Bible you find people who wept while praying only to see God answer their prayer.

Imagine what having the ear of God in your prayer life would do for your church, family and personal life. If we could get a world of Christians who would take these four steps to getting God's ear, we could change our world.

Jabez's Prayer

1 Chronicles 4:10

"And Jabez called on the God of Israel, saying, Oh that thou wouldest bless me indeed, and enlarge my coast, and that thine hand might be with me, and that thou wouldest keep me from evil, that it may not grieve me! And God granted him that which he requested."

One of the ways you can learn to pray is to read the prayers of the Bible, find out what they said, and see if God answered that prayer. If God answered a prayer for one of the people in the Bible, and if God is a just God, then God would have to answer the same prayer for us if we do everything that person who prayed did.

I find in the verse above one of the prayers of the Bible that moves my heart personally. According to the Bible, Jabez was born out of sorrow. What caused the sorrow the Bible does not tell us, but Jabez did not let the condition of his birth stop him from serving God. What I want you to see is the prayer which he prayed to God and what he asked God in this prayer.

First of all he asked God to bless him. There is nothing wrong with asking God to bless you when you pray. God is the One Who is the source of all blessing. So if God is the One Who is the source of all blessing, why not ask Him to bless your life? Certainly God wants to bless us, but we must not be afraid to ask God to bless us. Every Christian needs God's blessings if we are going to do anything worthwhile in this life.

Secondly, he asked God to *"...enlarge his coast..."* I believe this would be asking God to give him a bigger ministry. Though this may seem selfish, on a daily basis I ask God to enlarge the coasts of my ministry. I don't want my ministry to stay what it is right now, I want my ministry to grow and the influence of my ministry to grow. You should want the same for your ministry. In your prayers ask God to help the influence of your ministry to grow.

Thirdly, he asked God to put His hand upon him. How every Christian needs this in their life. To be very honest with you, many times I have told God that I would rather not live if His hand is not upon my life. Christian, God wants you to ask Him to put His hand upon you. Imagine what could happen in your life if you would ask God to keep His hand of blessing upon you? The need of every Christian is for God's hand to be upon them.

The last thing Jabez prayed for was for God to keep him from evil. Christian, every day of your life you should ask God to keep you, not only from evil, but also from sin. One of my daily prayers is that God would keep me from sin. I don't even want to have to face the temptation of sin, so if I can get God to keep me from sin, then maybe I will never have to face the temptation of sin. I just don't want to find out how strong I am against sin. If God can deliver me from sin, then I have a better chance of pleasing God, which is what I want to do. This should be your daily prayer as well.

Lastly, I love what the Bible says, "...And God granted him that which he requested." Imagine what your life would be like if this were your prayer, and God granted this prayer for you. Make this your prayer, and remind God how He answered this prayer for Jabez so that God will do the same for you.

A Strange Way to Minister

1 Chronicles 6:32

"And they ministered before the dwelling place of the tabernacle of the congregation with singing, until Solomon had built the house of the LORD in Jerusalem: and then they waited on their office according to their order."

As God goes through the genealogies of Israel, He stops in this verse to show us how some of these families ministered to others. God said their ministry to the congregation was through singing. I imagine the only ministry these people were involved with was singing in the services. Apparently if singing was classified a ministry by God, then singing must be important.

The word "ministry" means "an action or agency to aid people." In other words, ministering is not about helping yourself but helping others. So, when God said that singing was a ministry, our singing in the church services helps to aid the lives others. Let me give you a few quick thoughts concerning the ministry of singing.

First of all, singing should never take the place of preaching. Though I believe in singing in the church services, God later on in the Scriptures says it's through the *"...foolishness of preaching..."* that people are saved and helped. You should never have a church service where people sing and there is no preaching. Even though preaching is the most important part of the church service; singing is still an important part of the service.

Secondly, when the congregational songs are being sung, you should sing aloud heartily. You may not think you sound good, but you must understand that your singing is part of ministering to God's people. That means that everyone in a church service has a part in ministering to others through singing in the congregation. There is nothing like having an exciting song service where God's people sing aloud. It picks up the spirit of the people and helps in the preaching of God's Word.

Thirdly, you should find yourself singing throughout the day as a way to minister to those around you. It's important to listen to the right music because you want to sing music that will help people. I don't believe the rock music and country and western music of our day will help encourage the hearts of people. It is singing music about God that encourages people. You should be a person who has a song in your heart constantly for this ministers to the lives of others.

Lastly, you should sing songs regularly throughout the day because it ministers to your soul. When you minister to others it always helps you more than it will help them. If singing helps aid others, then I am positive that it will aid your soul as well. It is good to sing because you lift your spirit through singing. If you're down, try singing; it will lift your spirit. Singing should be a regular part of our day.

Let's never minimize the importance of singing. Let's realize it is a ministry in which anyone can participate. You ask in what ministry can you get involved? Try joining the ministry of singing; not in the choir or special music, though this is important, but sing in your church and in your daily life. Though this may seem like a strange way to minister, it is a ministry according to the Scriptures.

Responding Properly to Personal Treatment

1 Chronicles 12:17

"And David went out to meet them, and answered and said unto them, If ye be come peaceably unto me to help me, mine heart shall be knit unto you: but if ye be come to betray me to mine enemies, seeing there is no wrong in mine hands, the God of our fathers look thereon, and rebuke it."

The happenings in this passage of Scripture took place before David had become king. This was during the time when David was in Ziklag hiding from Saul. Saul had just been killed, and the men in this verse came to David to make him king over Judah.

We read in this verse two interesting statements that should help us in our responses to people who help us and to those who hurt us. Notice, David said that if they came to help him that he would knit his heart to them. But, then David said if they came to betray him to his enemies that he would let God repay them for their deeds. You will notice that when the people did him good, he felt it was his responsibility to do good back to them; this was David acting. But you will notice when others did him wrong, he felt it was God's responsibility to take care of these people.

In our lives, we will have people who do us good and people who will do wrong to us. In each case we are taught how to respond to these people. When people do good to us, we should do good back to them. We should never take for granted the good people do for us. When people go out of their way to help us, a "thank you" is always in order. Not only should we be thankful to these people, but I also believe we should do what we can to do good back to them.

Then when people do us wrong, we must be careful not to try and pay them back ourselves. Revenge is not our responsibility, it is God's. When people do us wrong, we must move on and let God deal with them. God sees what people do to you, and He will repay them according to their deeds. Too many people live their lives trying to get back at someone who has done them wrong, and the only one they are hurting by doing this is themselves. Even when we have done no wrong, we must leave it up to God to take care of those people who have wronged us.

Let me ask you a couple of questions. Have you done good to people who have been good to you? When is the last time you rewarded someone for the good they did to you? Don't be an ungrateful person! My other question is this, are you living your life trying to get back at those who have done you wrong? Let it go! Don't live your life in such a manner. This type of living causes you to be a bitter and angry person who no one will want to be around. Let's always be cognizant of these two areas in our lives, and watch that we treat others properly.

David's 3 Worst Decisions

1 Chronicles 21:8

"And David said unto God, I have sinned greatly, because I have done this thing: but now, I beseech thee, do away the iniquity of thy servant; for I have done very foolishly."

As great a man as King David was, at his best he was still a sinner. Likewise the same can be said about you and me. It matters not what position we hold, at our best we all are still sinners. Because of this fact, I can look at David's life and learn from his mistakes.

When I study David's life, I see that he made three major decisions that were wrong which had a major affect on his life. Let me quickly tell you about these three decisions. The first worst decision was when David copied the heathen's methods of serving God. In his desire to try and get close to God, he wanted to move the Ark of the Covenant to the city in which he lived. In his first attempt, he copied the method of the Philistines by putting the Ark on a new cart. A man died as a result of this decision. We must remember that compromise will always lead to bad results. In our lives and churches, we must be careful about trying to copy the world or the liberals in our service to God. We must realize that their ways are not the ways of God.

The second worst decision of David's life was when he decided to get out of his normal routine. This was when he committed the sin of adultery with Bathsheba. This sin started when he stayed home from the war instead of going to war as he usually did at that time of year. His decision to leave his routine led to horrible consequences in his life that affected him until the day of his death. Others died as well because of this decision. He was never quite able to escape the influences of this decision. Likewise, when we leave our daily routines, we set ourselves up for heartache. We must be careful about leaving the routines we have set up for ourselves and the routines God has set up for us. We must constantly watch that we don't make the same decision David made in leaving his routine.

The third worst decision of David's life was listening to his pride. In the verse above, we see his pride caused him to want to number his kingdom. This decision of giving in to pride led to the deaths of many people. Pride always leads us to wrong decisions. We must be careful about making decisions based upon how it affects us. We must realize in every decision we are not the issue, truth and right should always be the issue.

I want you to notice the common denominator in all of these decisions; death. Death is always the common denominator in sin. Sin's destination is always death, and we are not the exception to the rule. Guard yourself in these three areas of your life to make sure you don't make the same foolish mistakes David made. Realize if you do, you will have the same results in your life; death.

I Had in Mine Heart

1 Chronicles 28:2

"Then David the king stood up upon his feet, and said, Hear me, my brethren, and my people: As for me, I had in mine heart to build an house of rest for the ark of the covenant of the LORD, and for the footstool of our God, and had made ready for the building:"

I want you to think with me just a little bit, and be honest as I try to bring you to a conclusion. Imagine if someone came to you and gave you an envelope, and inside that envelope you saw a check for ten million dollars. After the shock was over, you now have more money than you've ever had in your entire life. Let me ask you, what is the very first thing you would do with that money? Let me pose this question another way. What would you do if you had a million dollars given to you? Let me put it yet another way just to try to get to a conclusion. If money were not an issue in your life because your financial resources were endless, what would you do with that money? Now think of these questions and write your answers down. The answer that you gave, the first thought that came to your mind if you had money is what is truly in your heart.

If these questions were posed to David, we have the answer in this verse as to what he would do. David would have built a house for God. That is what was in David's heart, and that is why God wanted to bless David so greatly.

The truth is what is in your heart is what you really are. What your answer was to the questions above is truly who you are. If you answered the questions honestly, you now know what's in your heart. What's even more sobering is God knows what's in our hearts. In verse 9 of this same chapter the

Bible says, *"...for the LORD searcheth all hearts..."* God knows what your answers are, and He also knows what you would do if He gave you that money. We may be able to lie to others, but we cannot lie to God for He searches our hearts.

I ask you, when I asked the questions to start this devotional out, did your first thought or answer have to do with God or you? If your first answer or thought had to do with you, then you are number one in your life and not God. Let's remember that God should be first in our lives. He demands and expects to be number one in our lives. Let's be careful about our desires and what we place at the top of our list of priorities. Let's work hard at making God the One Whom we place our desires upon. Let me say plainly, if He is number one in your life you will have more than you could ever want for God will bless you.

Ask God to help you to make Him the preeminent One in your life. Make your life about God, and you will see the same blessings in your life that David saw in his.

Have You Made an Altar Lately?

2 Chronicles 4:1

"Moreover he made an altar of brass, twenty cubits the length thereof, and twenty cubits the breadth thereof, and ten cubits the height thereof."

The importance of the altar in the Bible cannot be stressed enough. When you look at the altar, you will see there were many uses for it. For instance, the altar was a place of prayer; the altar was a place of sacrifice; the altar was a place of worship; the altar was a place where promises were made; the altar was a place where people turned back to God. Throughout the Bible anyone who left the altar left God. Those who used the altar normally kept themselves close to God.

As Solomon built the temple, the importance of the altar can be seen in the fact that God showed us how it was built, the size of it and the appearance of the altar. Apparently God thought the altar was important enough that He would tell us that an altar was made in this great temple which Solomon built.

We need to build an altar in our lives as well. One of the altars we ought to build in our lives is the family altar. What I mean by the family altar is that the family should daily have a time together when they pray to God and read His Word. The family altar can be a time that children will remember the rest of their lives if the importance of it is stressed and if it is done right.

Then I believe we ought to make a personal altar that we visit daily. What I am talking about here is a time when we daily come to God and spend time with Him. Simply put, every Christian ought to have a daily time of prayer with God; a time where we walk with God, confess our sins and ask Him for our needs.

Then the last altar I would like to discuss is the church altar. I believe every Christian ought to frequent the church altar. Too many Christians never use the altar at the church which is a big mistake. Every time a person stops using the church altar you can guarantee that person has started putting their eyes upon themselves. There is something humbling about going to the altar at church. You can give me every excuse in the world to try and justify your negligence of the altar, but it simply comes down to pride coming into your heart. The only reason you will not use the church altar is your pride.

Have you made an altar in your life lately? Have you used the family altar? Have you had your personal altar on a regular basis? When is the last time you used the church altar? Let's be careful to not forget the importance that God places on the altar, and let's use it so we can stay right with Him.

Fortifying the Strong Holds

2 Chronicles 11:11

"And he fortified the strong holds, and put captains in them, and store of victual, and of oil and wine."

After Rehoboam's great mistake of forsaking the advice of the older generation, in this verse he made a very wise decision that many seem to overlook. The Bible says that Rehoboam *"...fortified the strong holds..."* The strong holds were the places that were already strong. They were the areas of most importance in the defense of his country. If the strong holds went down, then the nation would go down with them.

In our Christian lives, many times we seem to focus more on our weaknesses than on our strengths. Though we should try to strengthen the areas of our lives that are weak, the one thing we must be careful about is not taking time to strengthen the areas of our life that are the strong holds, the pillars of our life. The reason I say this is because if the pillars of our life go down, then we will be destroyed. Trust me when I say this, Satan is not as concerned with your weaknesses as he is with your strengths. Satan knows if he can destroy the strong holds in your life then he can destroy you. Because of this, we should do in our lives what Rehoboam did in his kingdom and that is to fortify, or strengthen, our strong holds.

What are the strong holds of the Christian life? If I were to put my finger on the one area that I would consider our strong hold I would say our walk with God is the strong hold of the Christian life. It is amazing how much time many of us spend doing everything else God commands us to do but forsake the time of prayer and Bible study that is so necessary in the Christian life. In today's society we have become too busy for our own good. I hear people often say that they just don't have the time to pray and read their Bible. What a shame! If you lose your walk with God and your prayer time, you in essence destroy the very strong hold of the Christian life. No wonder so many Christians fall into sin when the strong holds of their lives have been forsaken!

I warn you to fortify the strong holds in your Christian life. Be sure daily to spend time praying and studying the Bible. Be careful that you don't get too busy to fortify the strong holds in your Christian life. Always remember, if your prayer time and Bible study time are forsaken, it won't be long before sin will creep into your life and destroy you. While trying to strengthen the weaknesses of our lives, let's not forget to fortify our strong holds of which the most important is spending time in prayer and studying the Bible.

You Are a Teacher

2 Chronicles 17:7

"Also in the third year of his reign he sent to his princes, even to Benhail, and to Obadiah, and to Zechariah, and to Nethaneel, and to Michaiah, to teach in the cities of Judah."

One of the greatest things you can do in life is to learn to teach others how to live a life that is right. Teaching is a powerful tool, for when you teach you influence lives both in the present and in the future.

Jehoshaphat realized the power of teaching and sent his princes out to teach the people. He also knew the best thing to teach the people was the Word of God. You see in verse 9 that these princes took the law of the LORD and taught the people. They did not teach them what their agenda was, but they taught them how God wanted them to live. I want you to notice the result of teaching the people in verse 10; fear fell on all the nations round about them. Teaching is a powerful tool, for with it we influence lives.

Whether you like it or not, you are a teacher. You are either teaching people to do right or you are teaching them to do wrong. Your goal in life ought to be to teach people to do right. The greatest thing you can do with your life is teach people to do right for nothing is more satisfying than knowing that you taught people the right way to life. You may wonder how we can teach people.

First, teach your children in your home. Parents, your daily life in the home should be about teaching your children the right way of life. Teach them from the Bible through devotions. Teach them from situations they face in life through truths from God's Word. Teach them the right and

155

wrong of society's problems. Don't waste the powerful tool of teaching in the home.

Secondly, teach people through the ministries of your church. One of the biggest reasons you should get involved in the ministries of your church is so that you can teach others. Get involved in the bus routes and teach children the right way to live. Make it a goal in your life to become a Sunday school teacher so you can teach people the right way to live.

Lastly, teach people with your life. The greatest teacher of people is the life you live. What you say with your mouth is important, but what you teach with your life is even more powerful. People watch the way you live and dress to see how they should live and dress. This is why we must be careful how we live our lives for we are teaching those who watch us.

Remember, you are a teacher to someone. Someone is watching you, and what you say and how you live is teaching them either right or wrong. Be sure to be a teacher of right so at the end of your life you can look back with fulfillment knowing you led people down the right paths of life.

Chameleon Christianity

2 Chronicles 24:2

"And Joash did that which was right in the sight of the LORD all the days of Jehoiada the priest."

Joash owed everything in his life to Jehoiada the priest. It was when Joash was a young man that Athaliah tried to kill Joash and all of his brothers, and he would have succeeded if it were not for Jehoiada the priest. Jehoiada, when he saw what was happening, took Joash and hid him and guarded him from the evil hands of Athaliah. He raised Joash as if he were his own son, and when Joash was old enough; he took over the throne of Judah.

A disturbing statement is made in this verse about Joash and that is he *"...did that which was right in the sight of the LORD all the days of Jehoiada the priest."* This is disturbing because he should have done right his whole life. Serving God and doing right was not about Jehoiada, it should have been about God. I see the same disturbing action among Christians today who seem to do right as long as they are with the right crowd. As long as they are in a crowd that does right, they will do right. When they get around someone else who is doing wrong, they don't have the backbone enough to stand up and do what is right. This is a shame! Christians should do right, not because we are trying to please man, but because we are trying to please God.

For instance, there are many students in Christian schools who seem to be good young people, but when they graduate and leave the good crowd, they end up living a worldly life. There are church members who, when they are around the church people, seem like they are good Christian people, but during the week, when they are around those with whom they work, they live like the world. Their language is filthy, their actions are worldly and their life has no resemblance of Christianity. Then there are other Christians who seem to do well as long as their pastor is alive. But, when the pastor moves to another pastorate or God sees fit to take him to Heaven, they end up changing what they believe or stop serving God altogether. What a shame that people would be this way. Who are they serving anyway? Are they serving the man or the God of the man?

Each of us must be careful that we do right, not because we are around right influences, but because right is right to do. Yes, we need to guard our influences and make sure we have the right influences in our life, but we should always do right whether the influences around us are right or not. If we can only do right because the influences around us are right, then what are we going to do when the time comes when there are no right influences? That day comes for everyone, for there will always be a time in our life when we are the only one who is doing right.

Watch yourself and make your actions those that are right because they are right to do and not because of the crowd. Always remember it is God Whom we serve and not man!

Encouraging Your Preacher

2 Chronicles 31:4

"Moreover he commanded the people that dwelt in Jerusalem to give the portion of the priests and the Levites, that they might be encouraged in the law of the LORD."

During the revival under Hezekiah's reign, the king commanded the people to give to the priest so that they could be an encouragement to them. What a strange commandment in the midst of revival. Yet the result of this commandment was the people obeyed and immediately started giving, not just money, but food as well. The people gave so much that the Bible says that there were plenty of leftovers. Then the Bible says in verse 10 that since the people began to give they *"...had enough to eat, and have left plenty: for the LORD hath blessed his people; and that which is left is this great store."* I want you to notice that God blessed the people for their giving to the house of the LORD and the priests so much so that they had plenty leftover for their own blessings. God always blesses giving, and He even blesses when you're giving to a man of God.

My purpose for writing this devotional today is to get you to see the importance of doing special things for the man of God. Your preacher has earned the right for you to do something special for him every once in awhile. Many people take their preacher for granted and never do anything special for him, which I think is unwise. Why should we do special things for our preacher? The Bible shows us in this verse; so we can be an encouragement to him. Would you like to be an encouragement to your preacher? Then you ought to do something special for him. Let me give you a few ideas.

On a regular basis you should write your preacher notes letting him know how much he has helped you through his preaching and counseling. You could also give your preacher a "crispy handshake" every once in awhile. What I mean by this is you put some money in your hand and shake his hand leaving him with a small gift. When you hear of a need your preacher has, you could either supply that need for him yourself or organize the church to supply that need. Another idea is once a year the church could buy the pastor and his wife each a new outfit. If you're struggling financially, you could always buy an extra bag of groceries when you go shopping and give it to him. Whatever you do, these gifts will be an encouragement to your preacher.

I challenge you this week to be an encouragement to your preacher. Find something you can do for your preacher and make it a personal or family endeavor to encourage him through a gift. I believe God will bless you for doing this because we saw in the verse above that God blessed His people when they took care of the man of God.

A Successful Influence for Christ

2 Chronicles 35:6

"So kill the passover, and sanctify yourselves, and prepare your brethren, that they may do according to the word of the LORD by the hand of Moses."

As Josiah prepared the people for the Passover, he gathered the Levites and taught them what they were to do to prepare themselves to administer the Passover. In the instructions, we find a recipe that will help every person to have a successful Christian influence on this world. Let me show you this recipe.

The very first thing necessary for a person to have a successful Christian influence is salvation. I know this may seem obvious, but the truth of the matter is I wonder how many people are in churches who do the works of God and are not saved themselves. No, I am not trying to get a bunch of results to brag about, but there are many people who down inside have doubts about their salvation. The very first thing a person who is going to be a good influence as a Christian must do is get saved. You cannot do God's work without the Saviour doing the work from within. Killing the Passover lamb was a picture of salvation as Jesus Christ is the Passover Lamb. There must be a time in your life when you have put your faith and trust in Jesus Christ to be your Saviour from your sins. Can you remember that time? Or, are you relying upon your knowledge of what you know a person needs to do to get saved? Or, are you even relying upon what one of your parents said that you did? This is not good enough! You must know for yourself that you trusted Christ. You should have a clear time in your life when you know that you trusted Christ as your Saviour.

The second thing necessary to have a good Christian influence is sanctification. Notice, Josiah told the Levites to *"sanctify yourselves."* Sanctification is setting you apart for a specific use. Every Christian should daily be setting himself apart for the use of God. Setting apart from what? Setting apart from the world and our personal agendas! Those who want to have a great influence upon the world for Christ's sake need to live like Christ would want them to live and not like the world. You will never have a great influence for the sake of Christ if you are living like the world. Likewise you will never be a great influence for Christ when your life is all about your agenda and what you want. Your life must be about living for God and what He wants. You must set yourself apart on a daily basis for this purpose.

The third thing necessary to be a successful Christian influence is soul winning. In this verse you will see they were to prepare their brethren. This is soul winning! A person who is going to be an influence for Christ must be a soul winner. You will never be the influence for Christ you need to be without being a soul winner.

Today, as you go about your day, be sure that you have done these three steps to be an influence for Christ. Be sure that you are saved. If you are not saved then take care of that today. Then set yourself apart for the service of Christ and go out and win people to Him. This is what will help you to be a successful influence for Christ.

Lose Those Stripes

Ezra 4:15

"That search may be made in the book of the records of thy fathers: so shalt thou find in the book of the records, and know that this city is a rebellious city, and hurtful unto kings and provinces, and that they have moved sedition within the same of old time: for which cause was this city destroyed."

The saying, "A tiger never loses its stripes" is a very true saying. What is meant by this saying is if a person has done a certain something before then they will most likely do it again because this is their habit.

That is very much the case with what we read in this verse. The enemies of the Jews did not like that Jerusalem was being rebuilt. Because of this, they sent a letter to the king and asked him to search the records and see what the habit of these people were. The reason for this is they knew what the habits of the Jews were, and they knew that this would cause the king to stop Jerusalem from being built. All of this was revealed because of the history of the Jews.

I wonder though, if there was a book of records about your life, what would we find about your normal routine or habits of life? One of the common pieces of advice I give to preachers as I travel is if a person is known to do something in the past, then they will most likely do it again. This is why you check the past of someone who you're considering hiring because if they were a bad worker in the past then they will be a bad worker now. A tiger never loses its stripes and a person always reverts back to their habits.

What is the habit of your life that people would find if they searched the records of your life? Would they find that you start something but never finish? Would they find that you're loyal for awhile and then become disloyal? Would they find that you're a person who is up and down in your disposition all the time? Would they find that you have a major character flaw when it comes to purity? Would they find that you're a person with whom it is hard to get along? Would they find that you're a person who regularly loses their temper? When I ask what they would find in your life, you know what they would find for you know what your habits of life are. You know what the "stripes" of your character are that you never seem to be able to change.

I say this for two reasons, first you should strive to be sure that the records of your life show good character habits. You don't want to be known for something bad! You should strive to be known as a person who can be counted on because your history shows that you can be counted on. Secondly, if the records of your life show some bad character habit, then determine to change your history. You may not be able to change your history over night, but you can start today to change your history. Though a tiger may normally not be able to lose its stripes, make the tiger lose its stripes in your life. Decide now that you are going to break the poor character habit that the records of your life reveal. Somewhere it has got to stop, and it might as well be right now.

Ask God to help you change that character flaw so you can serve Him better. Prove to people that you have changed. It's your choice as to whether or not you are going to change. Make the right choice so the records of your life reveal a good pattern instead of a bad pattern.

Thoughts Lead to Consequences

Proverbs 12:5

"The thoughts of the righteous are right: but the counsels of the wicked are deceit."

Your thought life could be the most important part of your life that you guard, for you are, or will be, what you think right now. God said that a righteous person has right thoughts. It's interesting that God did not say that the actions of the righteous are right, but that *"The thoughts of the righteous are right..."* God knew the importance of a person's thought life because thoughts lead to words, words lead to actions, and actions lead to consequences. Whatever your thought life is filled with right now is what you will be doing tomorrow. What you do tomorrow will carry consequences. So, in essence, though actions always lead to consequences, we could say that thoughts lead to consequences as well. If you want to do right in life then you need to have right thoughts, for a righteous person will have right thoughts.

I want you to notice something, if the thoughts of the righteous are right, then we better think on purpose. You will not think right thoughts by accident; you will only think right thoughts on purpose. What I mean by this is you must purposely force yourself to think right thoughts by placing yourself in the right situations which will cause you to think right thoughts. You will not have right thoughts by watching the filth that Hollywood puts out. If you are going to have right thoughts, then you must purposely read the right books, watch the right things, listen to the proper music and go to the right places. All these things control what we think.

Let me ask you, what is your thought life like? If I were to take your thoughts and publish them in these devotionals for

165

everyone to see, would you be embarrassed because of what you have been thinking lately? Remember, you are what you think! If you don't want to become what you are thinking then you need to change your thought life. Righteous people think right thoughts, and sinful people think sinful thoughts.

It all comes down to this, if you are having a problem with an area of your life then change your thoughts in that area, for you are what you think. Be careful about letting the wrong things control your thought life. Purposely take control of your thought life so you can think right thoughts that will make you do right actions, which will then result in good consequences.

Building and Repairing

Nehemiah 3:1

"Then Eliashib the high priest rose up with his brethren the priests, and they builded the sheep gate; they sanctified it, and set up the doors of it; even unto the tower of Meah they sanctified it, unto the tower of Hananeel."

One of the themes you see throughout the book of Nehemiah is the importance of building and repairing the walls. Several times throughout the third chapter you will see the words "build, builded, built and repaired." Most of the time, God talked about how men were in charge of repairing a portion of the wall that was torn down.

The Christian life is full of building and repairing. I think it is important for us to understand that in the Christian life God wants His people to be a people who build. God wants His people to be involved in building, for building will require people to grow. But, we also must be a people who are constantly repairing what sin has torn down in our lives.

I point this out because if you are going to feel satisfied in the Christian life, you must be involved in these two areas. You will never feel satisfied as a Christian without being involved in building something. It may be helping to build a ministry in your church or a life, but you need to get involved in building something. There is something very gratifying about looking back at something you have helped build and knowing you had a part in it.

Furthermore, you should be involved in repairing what sin has destroyed. Sin is a destroyer, and God's people should be involved in repairing that which sin has destroyed. I am talking about repairing the lives of the fallen. I am talking about repairing lines of beliefs that liberals have torn down. All of us should be involved somehow in repairing those whose lives have been ravaged by sin.

One other thing I want you to realize on this subject is that serving God is all about building and repairing when Satan is all about tearing down and hurting. We as Christians need to be careful that we employ ourselves in God's work and not in the work of Satan. What I mean by this is when we try to ruin people through gossip, or any other way that would destroy people, we are involving ourselves in the work of Satan. Let's be careful about this, for we definitely would not want to help his work.

I ask you in closing, what are you involved with that builds? Are you involved in your church and its ministries which build? Also, are you involved in trying to repair the lives of those whom sin has hurt and destroyed? Let's make it our life's mission to constantly be involved in both building and repairing.

Counted Faithful

Nehemiah 13:13

"And I made treasurers over the treasuries, Shelemiah the priest, and Zadok the scribe, and of the Levites, Pedaiah: and next to them was Hanan the son of Zaccur, the son of Mattaniah: for they were counted faithful, and their office was to distribute unto their brethren."

As Nehemiah came back to Jerusalem for the second time, he chose on this trip to make sure everything in the city of Jerusalem was set in order so that it could run smoothly in his absence. When you come to this verse, you see that he chose some men to be treasurers in the temple. When looking at the qualification of the men whom he chose, the Bible states that he chose men who *"...were counted faithful..."* Now I believe there are a few reasons he chose faithful men for this position, but what I would like to focus on is that the men were regarded as faithful men. These men were known by everybody to be men who could be counted on to be in their place of duty.

As we think of this, we should ask ourselves if people regard us as faithful. We should ask ourselves if people can count on us to be faithful to our duties. The word *"counted"* in this verse is the same word we use as being regarded or known as something. The word *"faithful"* means "to be constant in the performing of our duties." In other words they were dependable men who could be counted on to be there no matter what came up.

Every Christian should be known as a faithful, dependable person. We should be faithful to our duties and responsibilities. We should not be a people who always come up with excuses to get out of our responsibilities. We should not be a people who are absent from our positions when we are needed; but we should be the kind of people that no one has to worry about being where we are supposed to be. We should be faithful in our Sunday school class. We should be faithful in our church attendance. We should be faithful to our bus route. We should be faithful to the position we hold in our church. We should be faithful to our spouse and responsibilities at home. In all of these areas we should be regarded as people who can be depended upon to be in our place of responsibility at all times.

Make it a goal in your life to be counted faithful. Don't ever allow yourself to be a person who finds excuses as to why you can't fulfill your responsibility. Instead, be a person who finds excuses to be in your area of responsibility. One thing the world should always be able to say about God's people is that they can be counted upon to be in their place of responsibilities. They can always be counted upon to do what they said they would do. Be one who is counted faithful!

The Power of Disloyalty

Esther 1:16

"And Memucan answered before the king and the princes, Vashti the queen hath not done wrong to the king only, but also to all the princes, and to all the people that are in all the provinces of the king Ahasuerus."

We know the story very well. Vashti, the queen, was petitioned by the king to come and dance before him and his friends. Vashti refused to come and dance before a bunch of drunken, lustful men. I commend the decision on the surface for it seems that she would not be part of showing off her body to men who were not her husband. I don't know, and neither does anyone else, if this was the reason she would not dance before the king, but if this was the reason, she made the right choice.

Though we may justify the actions of Vashti, there is another truth we see in this verse that we can't pass up. You will notice that the Bible states in this verse, *"...the queen hath not done wrong to the king only, but also to all the princes, and to all the people that are in all the provinces of the king Ahasuerus."* Her disloyalty to the king, whether or not it was right, didn't just affect the king; it affected everyone in the kingdom.

Though we may think disloyalty is only between us and the leader, according to this verse disloyalty affects everyone who is influenced by the leader. The power of disloyalty is great! I have seen it in churches for years, but it doesn't just affect churches, it affects every realm in our society where leadership is involved. When a person chooses to be disloyal, they are affecting many people; many who are innocent will get involved in the disloyalty as well. We may think that being disloyal won't affect anyone else, but it always affects others.

When a person is disloyal to the pastor in a church, the power of their disloyalty will affect the whole church, and in many cases hurts the church and many who go to that church. When a person is disloyal on the job, it affects the morale of the workplace. This is why employees ought not to tell everyone of their disagreement with management. It is disloyal! It is not everyone's business what you and management are at odds about. I look in the sports world at disloyal team members. You see quite often that a player who is disloyal to the coach can literally ruin the whole season for their team because of their personal disloyalty.

When you have a problem with leadership, you should go directly to them to discuss your problem instead of airing your problem to everyone else. Even if you are right in your disagreement with leadership, you are wrong to be disloyal and air your disloyalty to everyone else. Disloyalty is very powerful! It not only affects many innocent people, but it will also destroy many bystanders.

Be careful about being disloyal. Don't be a part of disloyalty. If you have a disagreement, then talk directly to the one with whom you have the disagreement. If this does not work, then talk to God, the One Who can take care of the situation. This should be your first action anyway. Let's guard ourselves against disloyalty so that we don't ruin the innocent people who may see our disloyalty.

Facing Your Greatest Fear

Job 3:25

"For the thing which I greatly feared is come upon me, and that which I was afraid of is come unto me."

When you read about the life of Job, it is hard not to feel sorry for this man. You look at what he had, and where he ended up for a short time, and you really feel bad that a person would have to go through all of this. I don't mean to pile on Job, but you see him in this verse making a statement that I feel every person understands. Job said the thing he feared the most in his life actually happened to him. The thing that he was afraid of in life had come to him. As these things happened to him, the first reaction of Job was to feel sorry for himself. When you read the first few responses that Job had, you see him feeling sorry for himself and wishing he had never been born. Feeling sorry for yourself has never helped anyone, including Job. Job still had some things going for him even though his life seemed, at that moment, to be totally in despair.

What is it that you are afraid of in your life? What I mean by this is, what is that one thing you carry in the back of your mind that you hope never happens to you but you are afraid that it might? Is it some sickness that everyone in your family seems to have? Is it some situation that you see others around you facing? Let me give you a couple of thoughts that will help you when your greatest fear comes upon you.

First, it is not as bad as you think. Yes, Job's situation seemed pretty bad, but he still had several things going for him which I will point out. When your fear comes upon you, I promise you it is not as bad as you think it is. When that one thing you feared came upon the lives of others, they made it through and so will you. It is not the end of the world though at the time it may seem to be.

Secondly, you still have God's watchful eye upon you. At the end of the Book of Job, we see God responding to Job's questions. This means that God was watching him the whole time. Likewise, when heartache and sorrow come your way, God is still watching you. Do you realize the comfort this should bring that God has not forsaken you? As long as God's watchful eye is upon us, we should never despair, for God is still with us.

Thirdly, you are still saved. If you can take solace in anything during these times it is this, you are still saved. That which you feared and were afraid of cannot take away your salvation. That means you don't have to go to Hell. This alone should comfort you.

Lastly, if you're saved, you still have Heaven as your destination. What a comforting thought that the hardships that we face will all be over some day when we get to Heaven. Yes, that which you feared may have come upon you, but the worst thing it can do is usher you into a place of bliss; Heaven.

If today you are going through that thing which you greatly feared and were afraid of, take these pieces of advice and realize you can still make it. Job made it through his fears, and so can you. It was just a short portion of his life, and it is just a short portion of your life. Be careful not to let that which you fear and are afraid of stop you from serving God. Be careful that you don't fall into a life of self-pity. Keep going, God is with you!

Learn To Laugh

Job 8:20-21

"Behold, God will not cast away a perfect man, neither will he help the evil doers: Till he fill thy mouth with laughing, and thy lips with rejoicing."

One thing that I have learned as I travel is that Christians need to learn to laugh. Anyone who knows me knows I believe we ought to be serious about serving God, but I also believe that laughter is good for the soul.

Bildad, in his attempt to correct Job, makes a good statement from which we need to learn. In these verses he made a statement about God's treatment of the perfect man. He said that God would not cast away the perfect man nor help those who do evil until he fills his mouth with laughing. In other words, God often puts laughter in the mouth of His people. God does this because He knows how good laughter is for the Christian.

I believe one of the things that separate the Independent, Fundamental Baptist church from many other churches is the laughter. Many times when I am in revival meetings, I see pastors who will do things to make their people laugh; I like to see this! I think it is good for God's people to laugh. I think it is good for the world to see that God's people are happy and filled with laughter.

Laughter is a good medicine to help us through the rough times of life. It is those who never laugh who have the hardest times when hardships come their way. We should understand that God gave us a sense of humor. If God gave us a sense of humor then there is nothing wrong with laughing. I believe when we get to Heaven we will be surprised how much laughter we will hear.

Yes, there are times to be serious, but there are also times when we should laugh. The Bible says in Ecclesiastes 3:4 that there is a time to laugh. Again in Proverbs 17:22 we find that a merry heart is like medicine. Laughter is the medicine to the spirit and soul. Those who never laugh will have a soul and spirit that are sick. The way to help a person whose spirit is injured is to laugh. The way to help a person whose soul is hurting is to laugh. Laughter is the medicine that we apply to the hurting soul and spirit.

I encourage you to be a person who learns to laugh. Laugh at yourself when something funny happens to you. Laugh throughout the day when you hear something funny. Be a person who cheers a place with your laughter. People enjoy being around a happy person, and laughter is a sign of a happy heart. Yes, you may be going through rough times, but laughter will help take the rough edges off those rough times.

God Knows Your Way

Job 23:10

"But he knoweth the way that I take: when he hath tried me, I shall come forth as gold."

One of the more comforting statements in the Bible is found in this verse when it says, *"But he knoweth the way that I take..."* What a comfort it is to know that God knows where we are right now at this very moment. What a comfort it is to hold onto the fact that God, even in the midst of trials, knows the very paths that we are walking.

We must look at the verse prior to see the despair of Job's life before he made this statement. Before Job made this statement he said that he looked forward and backward and could not perceive the presence of God. He said that he looked on his left and right hand and could not find where God was in his life. Then we come to this verse to see Job, by faith, saying that though he could not see or find God, he understood that God knew the way he was taking even though God's presence could not be seen through his eyes.

So many times when we are going through trials that life brings our way, we find it hard to see God. Many times we can stand with Job and understand what he was going through at that moment, for many of us have been there as well. Yet we must by faith stand with Job knowing that God does know the way that we take.

What does it mean when it says that God *"...knoweth the way that I take..."* First of all, it means that God knows that way because He has walked that way Himself. Let me use Scripture to explain what I mean. The Scriptures say in Hebrews 4:15, *"For we have not an high priest which cannot be touched with the feeling of our infirmities; but was in all points tempted like as we are, yet without sin."* In other words, God knows the way we take because He has walked through the very thing that we are going through right now. It is not a strange way to God, for He has been there and understands what we are going through. God is not saying that He knows our way just because He is God; God is saying this by personal experience. What comfort it is to know that not only is God with us in trials, but He also knows by personal experience what we are going through.

Secondly, this phrase means that God knows exactly where we are right now even if we cannot see Him. Christian, you may not think that God is anywhere near you during your time of trial, but you must by faith realize that He will always be there. You, like Job, may not be able to see God, but I assure you through the authority of the Scriptures that God is very present.

Whatever you face today, realize that even if others cannot understand what you feel God can, for He has walked that pathway Himself. Whatever you are facing right now, be assured of one thing, though you may not see God, He is very present in your life and is there to help you during these times. Whatever you do, don't despair and don't give up. God knows the way that you are taking.

Loving Yourself

Proverbs 19:8

"He that getteth wisdom loveth his own soul: he that keepeth understanding shall find good."

I start out by asking you a very strange question. How much do you love yourself? Now before you answer, I know the "spiritual" answer would be that we are not to love ourselves. I don't want you to answer with the canned "spiritual" answer; I want you to answer what is truly in your heart. I believe if you answered truthfully, most would answer that they love themselves quite a bit. This may seem to be a selfish answer, but this is fact with most people for most of us love ourselves.

The problem with our canned answer is that when we say we love ourselves, this love is filled with selfishness. A love filled with selfishness is not a true love. The verse above says that if a man loves his own soul he will get wisdom. God then goes further and says that a man who obtains understanding will find good. So, if I love myself, I will get wisdom. If keeping understanding will bring good then what is wisdom and understanding? God shows us in Job 28:28 when He says, *"And unto man he said, Behold, the fear of the Lord, that is wisdom; and to depart from evil is understanding."* God says wisdom is having a fear of the Lord. In other words, God is teaching us that we don't really love ourselves if we don't have a fear of God. Why is that? This is true because without a fear of God we will do foolish things which will force God to have to punish us.

I look at our society and I see a society that has little to no fear of God. This is true in Christian circles as well. You can't tell me that a person would live like the world if they had a fear of God. You see, fear will cause you to be afraid of what the object of your fear can do to you. That fear will force you to be careful how you handle that object. For instance, a fear of electricity causes people to be extra careful when they are around it. A fear of heights will cause a person to use extra caution when forced to be around high places. Likewise a fear of God will force a Christian to do what God tells them to do out of fear of punishment from God.

You wouldn't miss church, if you had a fear of God. You wouldn't look at wrong websites, if you had a fear of God. You wouldn't talk about wrong things, if you had a fear of God. You wouldn't disobey the commands of the Scriptures, if you had a fear of God. A fear of God will cause all of us to live our lives according to the Scriptures.

So going back to the original question, how much do you really love yourself? The answer to this question is seen by how you live your life according to the Scriptures. I would advise you to love yourself. By loving yourself I mean; live your life with a fear of God which will cause you to live wisely and obey the Scriptures. The obtaining of wisdom from living in the fear of God shows how much you love yourself.

Opinions

Job 32:17

"I said, I will answer also my part, I also will shew mine opinion."

There is a danger in the answer of Elihu and many people are making the same mistake today. Elihu waited for the men who were older than him to answer Job, but after all was said and done, Elihu felt that Job had not been answered properly. As he started his answer to Job, he made the statement in this verse that he would also show his opinion. The truth is, Job did not need the opinion of man, what Job needed were absolutes from the Word of God. If someone would have answered Job from the Scriptures, then the Scriptures would have done their work in the heart of Job.

Too many times I find people who want to give their opinion instead of answering according to the Scriptures. I have always said, opinions are like arm pits, everyone has one and they stink. This world is filled with man's opinions when it needs to be filled with truth from the Scriptures. Let me give you a couple of thoughts about opinions.

First, never offer your opinion when you are not asked. Unsolicited opinions, or advice, are rarely heeded and often disdained. Too many times in a marriage a spouse wants to give their opinion only to cause strife in the marriage. Many times in the church Christians want to give their opinion only to cause problems for the pastor. Just because you have an opinion does not mean you need to give it. Unless someone asks you for your opinion, then the best thing you can do is keep your opinion to yourself.

Secondly, never offer an opinion in an area that is not your area. Even though someone wants your opinion of something, if they have no responsibility in that area, and you are not involved in that area, then you have no right to give your opinion. Many times people want you to offer an opinion about something that is not their responsibility hoping that you can back up their disloyalty. You need to be very stingy with your opinions. Only offer your opinion of an area out of your responsibility to a person who has responsibility in that area.

Thirdly, only offer opinions that are backed up with Scripture. Our opinions really do not matter. The only thing which truly matters is truth. Truth comes only from the Scriptures. Just because we have an opinion does not make us right. But if our opinion is backed up by Scripture, then our opinion carries authority with it. We must be careful about giving opinions that have no Scriptural basis.

Lastly, don't give an opinion about something you know nothing about. Nothing will make you look more foolish than giving an opinion about an area about which you have no knowledge. If you have no knowledge about something and someone asks your opinion, then simply tell them you have no knowledge about that area in which they want your opinion. There is no shame in not knowing something.

I say in closing, be very stingy with your opinions. Be careful to hold your opinion to yourself. Giving your opinion can make you look very bad if your opinion is not based upon truth from the Scriptures. Giving your unsolicited opinion can certainly ruin good relationships. The best thing we can do with our opinions is keep them to ourselves. This will keep you out of trouble.

God Can Do Every Thing

Job 42:2

"I know that thou canst do every thing, and that no thought can be withholden from thee."

There was a point in Job's life which he had to come to in order for God to be able to help him. What I am talking about is found in this verse when Job said, *"I know that thou canst do every thing..."* It was when Job realized that God did not need his help, and that he needed God's help, that God could help him. When Job came to the realization that God is the only One Who could help him out of his troubles, this is when we see God being able to bring Job out of the captivity of his trials.

I wonder if you have actually come to the same realization as Job did – that God can do everything. Do you realize that your marriage is not too far gone that God cannot repair it? It doesn't matter how damaged your marriage may be from years of fighting, God can do everything, which means He can salvage your marriage. Do you realize that there is no point when God can't repair your finances? I know we live in a day when it may seem that we are sunk financially, but remember that God can do everything. This would include getting you back on your feet financially. Do you also realize that even though your life may seem to be a mess, God can still do something with your life? It matters not how low in sin you have gone. God can do everything, including salvage your life from sin. You may be facing a health situation that to the doctors seems impossible to cure. Let me remind you that God can do everything including healing a body from sickness if He so chooses. You may have a child who has utterly ruined their life and has shut you off as a parent, but let me remind you that God can do everything including getting your child's attention once again.

Whatever it is that you face today, God can do everything. This includes the situation that you are currently facing. One of the biggest hindrances that keeps God from helping your situation is you. This may seem strong, but are you still trying to help God out with your situation? You will notice that when Job came to his end, and realized he could do nothing of himself to get out of his situation, it was at that moment God was able to bring him out of his troubles. It is when we come to the end of our rope and realize on our own we are completely helpless that God can step in and salvage our situation.

Whatever it is that you are facing today let me remind you, God can do everything. Stop trying to work it out yourself, and realize you have a God Who can help you with your situation. Let God do what He wants to do, and let him be the One Who helps you and brings you out of the captivity of your trials.

Beware of Temptation

Matthew 4:3

"And when the tempter came to him, he said, If thou be the Son of God, command that these stones be made bread."

One of the reasons Jesus came to Earth was to show us how to live. Jesus wanted to show us that it is possible to overcome this world and live a pure and holy life. The story in this verse is one of those times that Jesus used to teach us by example.

Jesus, being led by the Spirit into the wilderness, had finished His forty day fast. When the fast was over, we see that Satan came to Jesus tempting Him to sin. What is interesting is the timing of Satan's temptation. Satan chose to tempt Jesus in His weakest moment hoping to get Him to sin. Though this was Jesus' weakest moment, He still overcame the temptation of Satan.

One thing I constantly do is study myself. The reason being is the more I know about myself the better chance I have in being successful in the Christian life. I have learned that the greatest time of temptation for me comes at the same time that it came for Jesus. Satan is wise, and he knows when the best time is to tempt us to sin. Therefore, we must learn when it was in the life of Jesus that He was tempted and what He did to overcome that temptation.

There are two times in our lives when we must beware of temptation. The first time you must be very careful of temptation is when you are tired. You will notice that Jesus had just finished a forty day fast and certainly had to be physically weak and tired. We must guard ourselves when we are physically weak and tired. It is during these moments that Satan tempts us knowing that we don't have as much energy to fight temptation. Know yourself and when you are tired so that you can beware of temptation during these times. This is why it is important that we get rest, for when we have little rest our bodies and minds get tired, and we open ourselves to temptation. Watch yourself when you are tired so that you don't succumb to the temptation of the Devil. We must also watch ourselves when we are hungry. Lack of food will also lead to weakness. If you are fasting for a time, watch yourself as Satan will use this time to tempt you.

Now that we know when the temptation normally comes, what do we do to protect ourselves during these times? We do what Jesus did and that is to be led of the Spirit and use the Word of God. Simply put, spend time in the Bible and prayer. The Bible is our only weapon to fight against temptation, sin and Satan, and prayer gives us power to be led of the Spirit. If you don't have a personal time with God you have a greater chance of yielding to temptation.

Beware of Satan and his temptation when you are tired and hungry. Purposely tell yourself during these times to be extra careful not to yield to temptation. Read the Bible extra, and be sure to spend extra time in prayer during these times as well. In doing so, you will find yourself having the strength to overcome the temptation of the Devil.

Listen!

Matthew 11:15
"He that hath ears to hear, let him hear."

I have heard the statement over and over again, "God gave us two ears and one mouth because He wants us to listen twice as much as He want us to talk." To be honest with you I believe this statement is correct.

As Jesus preached to the disciples of John the Baptist, He said to them if they had ears, then listen. You will learn more by listening than you ever will by speaking. God's command to us today is still the same, listen! If we are commanded to listen, then to what are we commanded to listen? I believe that God wants us to listen to His Word through the preaching and teaching of It. Let me give you a few thoughts concerning listening.

First, if you are going to listen you must come prepared to listen. When going to church, you must come prepared to listen to the Word of God. This is through the preaching in the services and the teaching in your Sunday school class. Prepare yourself to listen by leaving anything at home that would keep you from listening. For instance, leave your cell phone and work at home. You are not coming prepared to listen when you come to church with everything else on your mind. Come to church with a prepared mind to listen to the preaching.

Second, pay attention to the preaching. Half of the reason we don't hear what is being preaching and taught behind the pulpit is because we just aren't paying attention. We let our minds wander as the preacher is preaching and then we miss what the preacher is trying to give us from God's Word. It takes character to listen, but you must make yourself listen on purpose to what is being said and not allow yourself to daydream during the preaching.

Third, listen to the preaching! I know it seems like I have already said this, but I wonder if people are actually listening to what is being said. Are you more interested in the jokes than you are in the truth of what the preacher is preaching? The preaching is what is important, not the jokes.

Then last of all, listen to the Holy Spirit. When the preaching is going on, the Holy Spirit is trying to speak to your heart. You must be sensitive to the Holy Spirit and listen to Him. Don't shut Him off when He starts speaking to you about something you need to change. Listen to the Holy Spirit and do what He tells you to do. Move to the altar in the invitation and change what the Holy Spirit has been talking to you about during the preaching.

I ask you, are you listening? Though I did not deal with these, are you listening to your authorities? Are you listening to the Sunday school teacher? Are you listening to your spouse? Are you listening to your parents? Are you listening to God? ARE YOU LISTENING? Remember, God said if we have ears that can hear then let them hear. Unplug your ears and listen to what is being said!

The Importance of Working Together

Matthew 12:25

"And Jesus knew their thoughts, and said unto them, Every kingdom divided against itself is brought to desolation; and every city or house divided against itself shall not stand:"

The story in the verse above is about some people who were concerned with a man who was possessed with a devil. Their concern for this man compelled them to bring him to Jesus for they knew He could heal this man of the blind and dumb devil. When the man was presented to Jesus, He healed this man so that he could both see and speak. The people were amazed at the power of Jesus and began to proclaim that Jesus was the Son of God. When the Pharisees heard this, their jealousy was evident when they accused Jesus of being a servant of Satan. Jesus response to this accusation is very helpful for us in many areas of life. His response was that a kingdom divided against itself cannot stand, but will be destroyed.

How true this is! A home that is divided against itself cannot stand. When a husband and wife are divided on the direction of their marriage, their marriage will most certainly fall. One of the reasons marriages break up is because they are divided in what they are trying to accomplish.

Parents who are divided against themselves in rearing their children will see their children destroyed in life. When rearing children, both parents **MUST** be in agreement on how to rear their children. If you have one parent who has one set of rules and another parent with another set of rules, you have a kingdom divided against itself which will bring destruction.

Likewise the same can be said about a church; if a church is divided against itself for whatever reason, then the church will destroy itself. You cannot have a successful church when the pastor wants to go one direction and the people want to go another direction. Everyone in the church must work together for the same cause if they want that church to succeed. This could also be said about a nation, workplace, organization or even friendships. Anything that is divided against itself will be destroyed.

We must work hard at whatever we are involved with to make sure everyone is going the same direction. We must be careful not to be the one who causes division in any of the areas mentioned above. Realize that the final goal which we are all trying to accomplish is greater than us having our own way. Work hard in whatever kingdom you are involved, whether it is your home, church, workplace, organization, team, school or friendship, so that you do your best to keep that kingdom from being divided against itself. Remember, a kingdom divided against itself cannot stand, so let's work extra hard at working together.

Your Purpose for Sacrifice

Matthew 19:27

"Then answered Peter and said unto him, Behold, we have forsaken all, and followed thee; what shall we have therefore?"

In this verse, I find the Apostle Peter asking Jesus an interesting question. He asked Jesus what he would get for his sacrifice of forsaking all. This question comes on the heals of a young man who claimed to be a good man and questioned the Saviour about what was needed to have eternal life. Jesus' final response to this man was, if he forsook all, he could have eternal life. This forsaking of all was Jesus telling this young man that he must forsake his self-righteousness and trust the righteousness of Jesus in order to get to Heaven. Peter though, was inquisitive about what a saved person would get for their sacrifice. Jesus told Peter that those who have forsaken all will receive a hundredfold blessing. In other words, it is impossible to out give God.

As I look at this story, I think of the Apostle Peter's question and am reminded of many Christians today. I am talking about many Christians who are so worried, as Peter was, about what they get out of their sacrifice. I believe too many of us are looking for God to give us something down here on Earth instead of receiving our blessings in Heaven.

I ask you Christian, what is your purpose for sacrifice? Is your purpose for sacrifice to receive accolades for what you have done down here on Earth? This is certainly petty and very selfish at the least. I'm afraid most people sacrifice so others will notice their sacrifice. Let me be very blunt, if your purpose for sacrifice is to get rewards here on Earth, then your purpose for sacrifice is very selfish. You shouldn't be looking for your rewards down here on Earth; you should be willing to sacrifice for the sake of Christ.

Let me go one step further on this thought. When you sacrifice, stop whining and complaining about what you are sacrificing. Too many Christians whine and complain about their sacrifice in the ministry. The truth is this, if you are sacrificing, then God promises to give you a hundredfold blessing for your sacrifice. So if you are not receiving the hundredfold blessing, then maybe you are receiving your reward for sacrifice by getting the pity of those whom you are around. To be honest, I would rather receive a hundredfold blessing from God than to receive accolades and pity from man.

In closing, look at your purpose of sacrifice and ask yourself why you are sacrificing. Are you doing it to receive man's praise, or are you doing it for the sake of Christ? Remember that God will reward you far more than you can sacrifice. So because of this, stop whining about what you have given up! Stop whining about what you are missing out on because of the ministry! Stop whining about the sacrifice you are supposedly making! Stop whining and complaining about all that you have to do! Realize if you are truly sacrificing for God, He is aware and will reward you for your sacrifice.

Cold Love

Matthew 24:12

"And because iniquity shall abound, the love of many shall wax cold."

You hear quite often that those who preach hard need to learn to love people because the need in our churches is for people to love each other. I agree that we have a lack of love among Christians. I agree that Christians need to learn to love each other. Loving one another is a command of God. But what is it that causes the love of people to weaken and become cold and indifferent?

Jesus tells us in the verse above that the cause of a lack of love is sin. God said that the increase of sin has led to the love of many growing cold. If you want love to increase then you must get sin to decrease. Too many times we think the way we can get people to love better is to preach and teach on loving, yet the truth is the way to get people to love better is to get them to forsake sin. Sin is to love what water is to fire. Sin is to love what cold is to hot. Sin is the damper of love; so to make love grow, we need to make sin shrink.

This is why we need preachers to preach hard against sin. Though preaching hard against sin may not seem to cause people to love each other, it is hard preaching that points out sin which causes people to get right with God. If people get right with God then people will love each other more.

Likewise, the same can be said to parents. If parents will enforce rules in their home, this will keep their children from doing wrong. The result of doing this is they will find that love will abound in their home. It is the parent who never enforces rules for their children to live by who lacks love for their children. When parents love their children, then they will enforce rules that will cause their children not to sin.

We have let society fool us into believing that the enforcement of rules is cruel and unloving, yet the opposite is true. It is the easing of rules which shows a lack of love by leadership. Doing right keeps you from sin which will keep you from the pain of sin's punishment. So if I truly love someone, then I will do all that I can to keep them from sinning. This means I should make sure as a preacher to preach hard against sin. This means as a parent I should make sure I am a part of a church that preaches against sin. Not just preaches against sin in general, but names sin and identifies it for us so we won't do it. This also means that as a parent I should make sure I enforce rules in my home so I can keep my children from doing wrong.

Let's never forget that the reason love grows cold is because of sin. If you find yourself lacking love for people, then you need to check your life and find the sin that is putting a damper on your love. Be strong against sin and you will find yourself having a strong love for others.

What Have You Done With Jesus?

Matthew 27:22

"Pilate saith unto them, What shall I do then with Jesus which is called Christ? They all say unto him, Let him be crucified."

As Jesus stood before Pilate when He was being tried, Pilate, not knowing what to do with Jesus, offered the chief priests and elders a deal. He gave them the choice to either release Barabbas, who was a hated thief, or to release Jesus. Out of envy and desire to see Jesus die, they chose to release Barabbas and have Jesus killed. Pilate, out of amazement, asked the question, *"...What shall I do then with Jesus which is called Christ?..."* This question that Pilate asked should be asked of every person alive, especially the Christian.

I ask you, what have you done with Jesus? Have you for the sake of a successful career chosen money and position over Jesus Christ, the One Who has saved you from your sins? I ask you, what have you done with Jesus? Did you choose the friends of this world over Jesus? What have these friends who try to get you to stop serving God ever done for you? I ask you, what have you done with Jesus? Have you chosen the hobbies and sports leagues of this world over Jesus? I am talking about those who on Sundays let their children play in sport's leagues instead of going to church. I am talking about people who participate in their hobbies instead of going to church. I ask you, what have you done with Jesus? Have you chosen yourself and your agenda over the desire that Jesus has for your life? What I am talking about are those who have run from the call of God on their life and chosen their own career for themselves.

195

SPIRITUAL ESPRESSO VOL 3

Before we ever sit and criticize those who chose Barabbas over Jesus, we had better look at our choices and see if we have made the same mistake. Many Christians daily choose something that will give temporal satisfaction over Jesus the One Who gives eternal satisfaction.

I implore you as you go throughout your day today to choose Jesus over anything else. Your choice of Jesus does not mean that you must not enjoy life, but your choice of Jesus should mean that He comes first in your life. In every decision we make, the question of what we will do with Jesus is involved. Let's make sure that we choose Jesus over anything else, for those who choose Jesus will see the greatest blessings from God upon their lives. When you are done reading this devotional, pray and tell Jesus that you choose Him today. Once you are done with this prayer, go out and live your day choosing Jesus in everything you do. Then tomorrow and everyday after that do the same!

A Prophet Without Honor

Mark 6:4

"But Jesus said unto them, A prophet is not without honour, but in his own country, and among his own kin, and in his own house."

In my travels throughout the years, one of the things I have noticed while driving down the highways are the signs that let everyone know someone famous was from that town. Usually the signs will say, "This is the childhood town of..." They do this so they can be identified with this person who has made, in their eyes, an impact upon society.

When Jesus went back to His home town, instead of being honored, He was criticized for the miracles that He performed. Can you imagine having Jesus live next door to you? Could you imagine saying that Jesus was one of your childhood friends? Could you imagine saying that you went to school with Jesus? Every one of these statements should have been an honor for these people in the town where Jesus grew up. Instead, they criticized Him for trying to do mighty works in their town. Jesus' response to this treatment is seen in the verse above when He said, *"...A prophet is not without honour, but in his own country, and among his own kin, and in his own house."* How sad that a prophet is honored in every other city but not his own.

Is this statement the case with those with whom you live and work? Let me illustrate what I mean. Is your husband a man who frequently helps others, but when he tries to help you he cannot because you won't listen to his advice? How sad that a man can give advice and help to others, but when he tries to help his own wife with the same advice it is turned away because she doesn't want her husband telling her what to do. Likewise the same could be said about a wife to her husband. Men, can your wife be a help to others, but when she comes to help you her help is turned down because she is your wife? I say to the children, do your parents help other children but can't help you because you don't want their help? Church member, can your pastor preach in other churches and the altars are filled and people want his advice, but when he preaches in his own church no one ever walks an aisle or ever comes to him for advice? What a shame that a person can help others, but their own family, church and kin reject the help because of their familiarity with this person.

The truth is this, of all the people that a person should be able to help, it should be those who are closest to him. Just because they are your spouse, parent, kin or pastor does not mean that you should ignore and reject their help. Of all the people who should honor someone, it should be those who are closest to them.

Be careful about not listening to those who are closest to you. When someone near you tries to help you, don't be so filled with pride that you won't allow their advice and help to be beneficial to you. Don't let the works of the one nearest you help others and not you because of your pride. You should be thankful that you have such a person in your presence.

Work hard at letting those who are near you help you. Don't be guilty of making your own "prophet" without honor in their own place. Honor them by letting them perform what God made them to do in their own country, city, family and church. Don't dishonor them by rejecting their help, instead honor them by accepting the same help that they would give to others.

Hearsay

Mark 14:58

"We heard him say, I will destroy this temple that is made with hands, and within three days I will build another made without hands."

One of the saddest commentaries about those who sentenced Jesus to die is that they sentenced Him to die based on hearsay. The religious leaders so badly wanted to destroy Jesus that they decided, based on hearsay, to convict Him even though the hearsay contradicted itself. When you look at the verse above you see the words, *"We heard him say..."* This is nothing more than hearsay. On these words Jesus was convicted and sentenced to die. It was due to hearsay that these people were willing to crucify the Saviour of the world.

Yet, I see the same thing happen today with people who in their minds convict people based on hearsay. There are many times when we will allow hearsay about someone to form our opinion of that person. I have heard people say things about Christian leaders based on hearsay that just plainly was not true. Normally, when someone tells me something negative about someone, I always ask them if they know this for a fact, or did they come to this conclusion because they heard this from someone else. We must be very careful about coming to conclusions about others based on hearsay. Let me give you some statements about hearsay to caution you so that you don't make the same foolish mistake these people made.

First, don't draw your conclusion about anyone based on hearsay. You must be careful that hearsay is not the evidence you use to form an opinion of someone. When you hear something bad about a person, don't let that bad that you heard be the only evidence you use in forming your opinion about them. Likewise, when you hear something good about a person, don't let that be the only evidence used to form your opinion about them. I know this is a strange statement, but whether good or bad, we should never form our opinion of a person based on any type of hearsay.

Secondly, when someone tries to get you to form an opinion about a person based on hearsay, ask them if they heard this themselves or if they know this for fact. Let me explain this statement to you. When someone says a person believes a certain way, always make sure you have heard them state that position from their mouth or read it in a book that they published. Too many times a person has a reputation that is built completely off the opinions that have been built by hearsay. Your best defense to keep you from looking foolish in this area is to ask a person who is trying to get you to make an opinion based on hearsay what proof they have. Put the pressure on the person making the accusation instead of just forming your opinion off hearsay.

Lastly, don't be guilty yourself of spreading hearsay about others. Too many times we fall trap to spreading hearsay about others. This action which we have done can literally destroy the name and character of a person. I would not, and neither should you, want to be part of destroying someone's name completely based on hearsay.

Be careful about forming your opinion on a position or a person completely off hearsay. Get your facts before you form your opinion. By doing this you will find yourself not being embarrassed by making foolish decisions. Always remember, hearsay is not fact. It is just what it says it is; it's hearing what someone said.

A Benefit of Overcoming Temptation

Luke 4:14

"And Jesus returned in the power of the Spirit into Galilee: and there went out a fame of him through all the region round about."

The verse above is the conclusion of the story of Jesus being tempted of the Devil in the wilderness. We know the story very well; Satan tempted our Saviour three times. In each of these instances when Jesus was tempted, He overcame the temptation with the Word of God. This alone is a lesson all of us should learn and remind ourselves of quite frequently. What I want you to see is the result of overcoming temptation. Notice in the verse above the Bible says, *"...Jesus returned in the power of the Spirit into Galilee..."* When did Jesus return in the power of the Spirit? He returned in the power of the Spirit after overcoming temptation.

If I asked the average Christian if they wanted to be filled with the power of the Spirit, I could just about guarantee that most Christians would answer in the affirmative. The problem is that though most Christians want to have the power of God upon their lives, they don't want to do what it takes to have the power of God. Let me explain this statement. Most Christians want the power of God, but they don't want to give up their sin in order to have the power of God. Not only will they not give up their sin, but they also will not spend time in prayer to get God's power upon them.

Christian, both of these are necessary in order to have God's power upon your life. One of the things that should motivate you to not yield to the temptation of sin is so that you can have God's power upon your life. It helps me when I am tempted to do wrong to remember that by not yielding to temptation I can have God's power upon my life. I realize that if I yield to temptation I, by my actions, quench the Holy Spirit of God. I so desperately don't want to do this, so this thought motivates me not to yield to the temptation. My desire to have God's power on my life is greater than the desire to have what the temptation of sin offers.

This is one of the keys to overcoming sin. Your desire to have God's power MUST be greater than the desire to have what the temptation of sin offers. Listen, God's power on your life will allow you to do greater things for God. God's power will allow you to help people in a greater way. God's power on your life will allow greater works to be done through you. But on the contrary, sin in your life will rob you of God's power. Sin in your life will steal your joy. Sin in your life will bring God's judgment and not His power. The end of sin is never what it promises, whereas the power of God on your life is always more than what you can imagine.

I don't know what the temptation is that you face quite frequently, but remember that by not yielding to this temptation you can have the power of God upon your life in a greater way than by yielding to the temptation. As the song says, "Yield not to temptation..." Why? Don't yield to temptation, if for no other reason, so that you may return from that temptation with the power of the Spirit upon your life.

Jesus, Your First Option

Luke 7:4

"And when they came to Jesus, they besought him instantly, saying, That he was worthy for whom he should do this:"

This verse comes from the story of the centurion whose servant was sick and ready to die. This centurion, who cared so much for his servant, knew that Jesus was the only One Who could help his servant. This verse says that when Jesus came to town that the centurion *"...besought him instantly..."* to heal his servant. I love that the centurion instantly sought for Jesus to do something to help his servant. He did not use Jesus as a last resort, but he used Jesus as his first resort and first option. He didn't wait until he had visited every doctor in town to get help from Jesus; he went to Jesus *"instantly"* to get help. He realized the One to go to and get help for his servant was the One Who could help his servant, and this was Jesus.

I wonder how many times we wait to come to Jesus when we ought to make Him our first option for help. I fear too many times that Jesus has become a last resort in our lives. This should never be the case! Jesus should be the first One we seek to get help with our problems. In fact, Matthew 6:33 commands us to go to Jesus first when it says, *"But seek ye first the kingdom of God, and his righteousness; and all these things shall be added unto you."* God promises help when we come to Him first.

When you are having marriage problems, go instantly to Jesus to get help for your marriage. Stop trying every marriage book and counselor, and run to Jesus and ask for His help in your marriage. When you are having financial problems, go instantly to Jesus to obtain His help with your finances. You ought not run to the financial gurus first to get help; you ought to go to Jesus first to get help. When you're having health problems, before you go to the doctors and spend thousands of dollars, go first to Jesus and ask for His help with your health. I am not against you going to the doctor; I am against you going to the doctor first and Jesus last. The problems America faces today could be helped if she would instantly run to Jesus; He has the answers for America's problems.

Whenever you are faced with a problem, whether it be wisdom for a job situation, health, family issues, economic issues, spiritual issues, relationship issues or any problem that has not been mentioned, always remember to instantly go to Jesus with your problem first. Don't let Jesus become your last resort. Make Him the One Whom you instantly run to when problems come your way in life. It matters not how big or small the problem is, take it instantly to Jesus, He is your answer!

Relationships with God

Luke 15:31

"And he said unto him, Son, thou art ever with me, and all that I have is thine."

One of the more popular parables in the Bible is the parable of the Prodigal Son. In this parable, a young man demanded that his father give him his inheritance. The father reluctantly did so only to see his boy leave and waste his money living in the world. When all was gone, this young man found himself feeding swine. Realizing how foolish he had been, he decided to go back home and work for his father. When he arrived back home, the father rejected the son's offer to be a servant and instead took him back as his son. I find five different relationships displayed between the prodigal son and the father that every Christian will find themselves having with God.

The first relationship we find is a strained relationship. In verse 12, a strained relationship developed because the son demanded of the father his inheritance. This is a relationship where the Christian demands of God to give them something for the works they have done. They feel that God owes them because of what they have "sacrificed." This strained relationship is a poor relationship to have with God. You feel God owes you when in all reality you owe God. A demanding spirit is what causes this strained relationship.

The second relationship is a distant relationship. In verse 13, the son left home to go live his own life. What a sad relationship to have with God! God's lifestyle brings blessings. Because too many Christians feel they are missing out on all the fun, they go and live in the world trying to have the fun the world offers. This relationship with God only leads to heartache. This relationship with God is established because a Christian will not give up their sin.

The third relationship is a servant relationship. Notice in verse 19 the son simply wanted to be a servant for his father. Now there is nothing wrong with this relationship with God, but this is not the best relationship you can have with God. This is the Christian who serves God and does right because they are supposed to live this way. They work for God out of obligation because God commands them to do so.

The fourth relationship I found is a close relationship. You will find this relationship displayed in verse 24 when the father says to the son that he would not accept him as a servant, but still considers him his son. The Christian in this relationship with God has moved from being a servant in their actions to realizing they are a member of God's family. They now approach God as a Father and not as a Master. They now serve God out of love and not out of obligation. They now want to do right to please their Father and not to please their Master. There is no shame at all in this relationship.

The best relationship you can have with God is found in verse 31, a trusted relationship. This is a relationship where you have proved to God after all you have gone through together that you are still loyal and serving Him. This relationship is established by going through hard times, and still you are serving God with love and enthusiasm. In this relationship, God trusts you. This is the best of all relationships! Not only do I want to have that close relationship where I serve God out of love because He is my Father, but I also want that relationship where God trusts me because I have always been with Him no matter what came our way.

I ask you, which relationship do you find yourself in with God? Strive to achieve that trusted relationship, for this relationship is where you trust God and God trusts you. It is also where you will find that the greatest blessing you have is your relationship with God.

Good Habits

Luke 22:39

"And he came out, and went, as he was wont, to the mount of Olives; and his disciples also followed him."

One of the greatest attributes of Jesus that we learn from the Scriptures is that He was a man of routine. We notice in the verse above that Jesus was going to the Mount of Olives which was His custom, routine, or habit. The phrase, *"as he was wont"* means *"as his custom or routine."* It was a habit for Jesus to go to the Mount of Olives to pray. It was something that everyone knew about Jesus. Apparently people must have seen Jesus pray there quite often for everyone to know this was His habit.

My question for you is this, for what habits are you known? What is it that everyone knows is your habit or routine? It ought to be everyone's desire to be known to have good habits. Good habits not only protect you from yourself, but good habits will also protect you from others.

This reminds me about a young lady who wanted to date me when I was in high school. She came to me one day and told me that she wanted to date me but knew that I would never date her. She said that she knew that she was not the type of girl that I would date. Her reason for saying this was because those around me knew what my habits were.

We should work at having good habits. Good habits will keep us from getting ourselves into trouble, but good habits will also show others what we will and will not do. We ought to become predictable about what we will and will not do. I know some think this is not good, but if Jesus made His habits known, then I would think we ought to make our habits known as well.

Let me ask you, first of all do you have habits that you do all the time? Are you a person who routinely does the same thing over and over again, or are you a person who only does what the moment dictates? If you are a person without habits, you are sure to hurt yourself in the long run. Secondly, if you are a person of habit, are your habits good habits? I believe it is very important for you to have habits, but the habits you have should be good habits. These good habits will protect you from others trying to tempt you. Don't try and hide your habits but let them be known. This is a protection for you!

Make it your goal that people know you as a person with good habits. Habits such as: going to church, helping others, reading your Bible and praying, being loyal to authority and being a hard worker. These are just a few of the good habits for which we should strive, but you should be known as a person with good habits.

If the verse above was about you, would the verse say that you are a person of habit or would the verse say that by chance you went to the Mount of Olives? Write some things down that you want to make your habits and then start doing them all the time so you can be known as a person of habit.

Which Way Do You Lean?

Proverbs 3:5-6

"Trust in the LORD with all thine heart; and lean not unto thine own understanding. In all thy ways acknowledge him, and he shall direct thy paths."

Nothing changes a person's life more than a decision. Making the right decisions in life seems to be one of the hardest accomplishments a person will ever achieve. Sometimes, when we make decisions, the decisions that we make are not going to be easy decisions. For instance, sometimes the decisions we make, even if they are the right decisions, will hurt those whom we love. There are other decisions that we have to make when we must choose between right and right. Then there are decisions in life that we must make that just don't seem to have a clear cut option in which to take. Because of this, we need help when it comes to our decision making.

In my life one of the passages in the Bible that has helped me in making decisions are the verses above. God directs us, when it comes to making a decision, to trust the LORD in that decision we must make. He also tells us that when we make a decision, we need to acknowledge Him on every path of that decision. But I want you to notice a small phrase in verse 5 which says, *"...and lean not unto thine own understanding."* Most of the decisions which we will make will lean towards one direction. God says that when we make decisions we need to be sure that our decisions lean towards God and not towards ourselves.

One of the things that will help us to learn how to make decisions is to study our past decisions. The reason we study our past decisions is to learn which way our decisions seem to lean. We will learn a lot about our decision maker by studying our past decisions. We will learn if our decisions seem to lean towards what the LORD wants us to do or towards our own understanding.

Now that you have learned which way your decision maker seems to lean, you must now keep that in your mind when it comes to future decisions. What I mean by this is that if our decision maker seems to make decisions which lean towards our own understanding, then we must be cognizant that we must push ourselves and our desire out of the decision making process. You see, decisions should not be made by how they affect us; decisions should be made by how they affect God. This is why our decision maker seems to lean towards our understanding because our decisions are about how they affect us. If you want your decisions to lean towards how they affect God, then you must train yourself not to make yourself the issue in the decision making process.

Finally, when it comes down to making the decision, be sure that your decision leans towards what God wants and not what you want. Though at times you may not understand this, you must trust God that He knows what is best for you. He has never done anything to hurt you in the past, and He will not change His ways of treatment towards you now.

Let's learn to make our decision lean more towards God than they do towards us. Our ultimate goal in decision making is to make all decisions lean towards God. Until then, be aware of which way your decision maker seems to lean, and purposely make a decision that leans towards what God wants and not towards your understanding.

Evidence for Validation

John 10:37-38

"If I do not the works of my Father, believe me not. But if I do, though ye believe not me, believe the works: that ye may know, and believe, that the Father is in me, and I in him."

According to the Bible, the Jews were a people who required a sign in order for them to believe that someone was from God. As Jesus preached to them, their hatred for Jesus grew and their skeptical attitude towards Jesus grew even greater. In the verses above we see Jesus tried to get these people to believe that He was the Son of God. He tried to use His title as the Son of God to prove the evidence of His authority. But we can see these people did not believe in Him just because He claimed to be the Son of God. So, He came to the final evidence that they could not deny and these were His works. Jesus said that if they would not believe Him because of Who He said He was, then at least look at His works and believe Him because of His works.

I look at this and notice that this is what anyone must have in order for others to believe in your position and follow you. A title doesn't really mean much to people. Just because you carry a title does not mean that people should automatically follow you. One of the greatest mistakes I see from young leaders is that they demand loyalty and trust because of their title. The truth is most people could care less about what title you hold. Even our own teenagers don't care about our title of parent. This is not right, but this is sometimes fact. The one thing that is always hard to dismiss are the works that God does through us. Every follower needs to see your works in order to validate your position of authority. Jesus had these works to validate His position, and this is why He could tell the Jews to at least look at His works.

I ask the reader, what works do you have that validate what you say and the position of authority which you claim? As a soul winner, the works which you can claim are the proof of changed lives. Though people may not want to believe in what you are telling them, the one thing they cannot discredit is what Jesus has done in your life since you got saved. Your works validate what you are saying about salvation and give you authority to tell others the truth of salvation.

If you are a leader of some sort, you had better have some works to validate you holding that position. Most followers will despise you holding that position until you have some works to prove that you deserve that position. If you do the same amount of work as those who follow you, then you have not validated your right for respect of your position. You as a leader must out work your followers and accomplish more work than they do. By doing so, you validate your position which will then cause followers to want to follow you because they will want to do what you have done.

To every parent who reads this, you better have some works which your children can see that validate your right for them following you. Don't get me wrong, they are to follow you no matter what because the Bible commands them to do so. But if you can prove to them through your works and what you accomplish in your life that they need you, then you will find that your works validate your position.

Each of us, whether we hold position or not, need to look at our lives and see if we have any works which validate what we are doing. As a Christian, you need works to validate your claim to the world. As leaders, you need works to validate your claim to followers. Because of this, we should be busy doing the work of God, for when we do His work, and He works through us, then those works which God does will validate our position and give us authority to lead others down the right pathway of life.

Position Must Be Earned

John 13:16

"Verily, verily, I say unto you, The servant is not greater than his lord; neither he that is sent greater than he that sent him."

One problem I see quite often in our society is the mentality among people that they don't want the next generation to have to go through what they went through when they were younger. On top of this, I see the present generation who want position handed to them without going through the school of hard knox that those before them went through. The mentality from both of these positions is destroying our nation.

The story in the verse above comes from the last supper that Jesus had with His disciples. After the supper was over, Jesus took a basin of water and washed the disciple's feet. After washing their feet, Jesus told them they were to do to others what He did to them. Simply put, Jesus was teaching His disciples to serve others instead of expecting others to serve them.

But the one truth I want you to see is in the verse above is that Jesus told His disciples, *"...The servant is not greater than his lord; neither he that is sent greater than he that sent him."* What Jesus was trying to get across to His disciples is that they have no right to just have everything handed to them. He wanted them to learn that if they wanted what He had then they were to go through what He had to go through to get where He was.

I wish parents would learn this truth for the sake of their children. Parents, your children need the hard times to make them into the kind of people you want them to be. Too many times as parents we don't want our children to have to suffer like we did growing up, but it was those hard times that made us who we are today. A parent who tries to keep their children from going through tough times like they went through is only hurting them. Your children need the tough times so they can become what God intends for them to become.

Let me take this into one other realm. Every follower who reads this should not expect position to just be handed to them. I am a big believer that everyone should earn their way into a position. Just because your parents hold position does not mean that you should inherit that position. No, you should earn that position just like they had to earn it. Every follower should realize that they are not above any job. If those in position of leadership had to clean the toilets when they were in your position, then you should have to do the same. All I am trying to say is that the servant is not greater than his lord. If your leader, boss, parent, pastor or authority had to go through hard times to get where they are, then you are not better than they. You should earn your way, and work your way up the ladder just like they did.

Be careful about thinking you are above a job. You are never above any job! As a follower, don't expect position without going through the hard times your leader had to go through to get that position. As a leader, don't allow the follower to get position without going through the hard times like you did. As a nation, we must not think that we shouldn't sacrifice for the next generation like previous generations sacrificed for us. As a nation we need to realize that we must sacrifice for the next generation if we want to be considered a great generation. Let's not expect any position let's earn it!

Thoughts About Peer Pressure

John 19:16

"Then delivered he him therefore unto them to be crucified. And they took Jesus, and led him away."

Peer pressure is a real thing that not only affects teenagers but adults as well. For someone to think that peer pressure is only for teenagers is to have their head in the sand. When you look at the political world, most of the decisions politicians make are because of the influence of peers. When you look at the world, most of the things adults do that are wrong are done because of peer pressure. Hollywood actors have their beliefs and live their lifestyles the way they do mainly out of peer pressure. Even in the Christian world, many preachers, as well as church members, do what they do out of peer pressure.

The verse above comes from the time when Jesus stood before Pilate to be tried. After Pilate questioned Jesus about the accusations that were thrown at Him, Pilate came back to the people and announced that he found no fault in Jesus. The people, being influenced by the chief priests, cried out to crucify Jesus. They even threw into the face of Pilate that if he released Jesus that he was not a friend of Caesar. Here they are trying to use peer pressure to get Pilate to do what they wanted him to do. As we can see from the verse above, Pilate yielded to the peer pressure and delivered Jesus to be crucified.

Peer pressure in itself is not bad. Like everything else, Satan always takes the good and perverts it to make it bad. Peer pressure used in a right way will cause people to do right. But, peer pressure used in a wrong way will cause people to do wrong. Let me give you a few guidelines concerning peer pressure.

217

When peer pressure tries to lure you to make an immediate decision, don't listen to the peer pressure. Immediate decisions most of the time lead to heartache. Almost everything that is worth doing can wait for you to think through the decision. When peers try to pressure you into making an immediate decision, decline to give in to the peer pressure.

Secondly, when peer pressure is being applied, look at the end result of the decision to decide whether you should do what your peers want you to do. Instead of yielding to your peers so that you can be accepted by them, you would be better off looking at the end result and the consequences that you will have to live with the rest of your life. I guarantee it, if Pilate would have looked at the end result of being the ruler who crucified Jesus, he never would have made that decision. Remember that every decision made has consequences with that decision. Don't let your peers pressure you into making a decision when you know you will hate living with its consequence for the rest of your life.

Last of all, when peers try to pressure you to do right, yield to that pressure. Every one of us should place ourselves in an atmosphere of peers who will pressure us to do right. This action will force most of us to do right longer than trying to do right on our own. I know we should have the character to do right, but because most of us don't have that type of character, place yourself in the midst of peers who will force you to have the character to live right. This thought alone will change your behavior and actions for right more than anything else ever will. If you want to do right the rest of your life, then place yourself among peers who will pressure you to do right.

Remember, peer pressure itself is not bad, it is what kind of peer pressure we yield to which determines whether it is bad or not. We ultimately decide what kind of peer pressure we will daily face by the friends we choose. Therefore, choose your friends wisely so you will only face peers who pressure you into doing right.

Doubting God's Miracles

Acts 2:12
"And they were all amazed, and were in doubt, saying one to another, What meaneth this?"

A sad statement is made about these people in the verse above when the Scriptures say, *"And they were all amazed, and were in doubt..."* Two phrases that seem to contradict themselves, the first phrase is they were amazed at what was happening in their presence only to be followed up with a second phrase that says they doubted what they saw. This is sad because these people, who were being preached to, knew the Scriptures. According to verse 16 and 17 of this same chapter, they had read in the book of Joel that what was happening in their presence was the fulfillment of prophecy. You would think that instead of doubting they would rejoice that they were seeing prophecy fulfilled before their own eyes. But as we read, doubt wiped out any rejoicing that should have been done.

This happens quite often among Christians today. We often read in the Scriptures promises from God that if we will do something, He will reward our actions with blessings and miracles. So what happens is people and churches obey the Scriptures, and in return, God blesses them for their obedience. As always there are doubters who see the blessings and criticize, as these people did, the blessings and miracles of God upon a person or church.

I ask you, do you doubt when God is doing a work? For instance, when your church is seeing the blessings of God with souls being saved and growth of attendance, are you one of the negative doubters who asks how long this is going to last? Instead of doubting, you should be rejoicing that God is blessing your church. Instead of doubting, you should be involved in the works that caused God to bless your church.

Likewise in a person's life, when you see God blessing someone's ministry or life, are you the one who doubts that person and what God is doing through them? Are you the one who stands criticizing this person because of your doubt?

Doubt is like a disease that spreads. When one person doubts and expresses their doubt to others, that doubt will begin to spread causing others to doubt. So when you doubt the miracles of God and express your doubt to others, you are guilty of spreading something that could very well stop the very miracles and blessings of God in your presence.

Be careful about living a life of doubt and always questioning what is happening in a person's life or in a church. I would hate to think, that like these people, you miss out on God's promises proclaimed through prophecy because of your doubt. Instead of doubting, rejoice and get involved in the works that are causing such blessings. Don't be negative and spread your doubt, get involved and be a part of the miracle that you are seeing in your church and in the lives of others.

Good Works and Almsdeeds

Acts 9:36

"Now there was at Joppa a certain disciple named Tabitha, which by interpretation is called Dorcas: this woman was full of good works and almsdeeds which she did."

One action that always seems to get the attention of society is when people give their finances to help those in need. I think of catastrophes that have happened around the world where people give of their own money to help others who are in desperate need of help.

Tabitha was a lady in the church who seemed to be a person who gave her life to help others. We read about this lady in the passage where the verse above is found, and see that she was sick and eventually died because of the sickness. Upon her death, certain disciples sent for Peter to come so that he could ask God to give this dear lady life again. It was very evident how many people she had helped by the amount of people present and weeping because of her death. When Peter came, he prayed to God, and God gave her life again.

What I want you to notice about Tabitha is that God described her as a lady who was *"...full of good works and almsdeeds..."* Notice that good works and almsdeeds are two different things. There are several instances in the Bible where God will describe a word with another word or phrase after that word so that we can understand what He was talking about. This was not the case with these words as you see these words are separated by the word *"and."* In other words, not only was she full of good works, but in addition to her good works, she was also full of almsdeeds.

"Good works" is "an act of service given to meet the needs of God." In other words, this lady's life was filled with works to make sure God's needs were met. You will notice that these works were mentioned before the almsdeeds. I believe the reason why is because serving God should always be the first thing we do in our life. Our service to do good works should be to meet the needs of God.

Almsdeeds is different from good works in that almsdeeds is "an act of giving to meet the needs of man." It is interesting that this woman's life was filled with giving. She gave of her life to serve God to meet His needs, but in addition to this, she also gave of her life to meet the needs of man. In all reality, this is what life is all about; giving of our life through works to meet the needs of God and giving of our finances to meet the needs of man. If a person will spend their life trying to meet the needs of God and man, I believe they will find themselves a happy person.

One other thought is this, she didn't just have one of these attributes, she had both attributes. Normally a person who gives of their time to serve God with their life is not a great giver to meet the needs of man financially. The same can be said about those who give of their finances to help others. What God wants from His people are a people who are filled with both; giving of your life to meet His needs and giving of your finances to meet the needs of man.

I ask you, is your life filled with good works and almsdeeds? Do you see yourself lacking in one of these areas? Make it your daily goal to meet God's needs through living for Him, but also make it your goal to help someone everyday. I believe you will find yourself feeling fulfilled in life if you will do both.

Have You Separated?

Acts 13:2

"As they ministered to the Lord, and fasted, the Holy Ghost said, Separate me Barnabas and Saul for the work whereunto I have called them."

As the work of God flourished in the early days of the church, God wanted to send Barnabas and Saul to other cities to bring the Gospel to the Gentile world. God told the church to separate Barnabas and Saul for this work. It is interesting that God told the church to separate these men, because without a person being separated they will never accomplish anything great for God.

Too many times in a person's life we see they want to serve God, but don't want to separate from those things which will hold them back from serving God to their fullest potential. In fact, sometimes the things from which a person must separate are not bad, but will hold them back from doing the work God wants them to do. God will never use you to the extent which He desires to use you without you separating yourself as Barnabas and Saul were separated.

If we are going to be used of God in a great way, we must first separate ourselves from the world. When I say from the world, I am not just talking about the world's lifestyle, though we must do this, I am talking about the world meaning the affairs of this world which we are tied into. Let me explain, several years ago when I stepped out to go into full-time evangelism, I realized that God could never use me until I left my job and worked full-time as an evangelist trusting God to take care of my needs. When I stepped out into full-time evangelism, I quit my job and served God full-time. Many people want to have the world and service to God, but if we are ever going to be used by God, we must not be entangled in the affairs of this life.

There is a second area from which we must separate ourselves if we are going to be used by God and this is our personal desires. There are many times when our personal desires get in the way of God's will for our lives. If you want God to use you then you must burn your personal desires and let God have His desires.

Do you want God to use you? If you do then you must separate yourself from the world. You must not be so entangled in the affairs of the world that God's work takes second place in your life. Also, if you want to be used, you must set your personal desires aside for the sake of His desires to be fulfilled. Without separation in these areas, you will never reach the potential in God's will for your life.

Repentance Brings Action

Acts 19:18-19

"And many that believed came, and confessed, and shewed their deeds. Many of them also which used curious arts brought their books together, and burned them before all men: and they counted the price of them, and found it fifty thousand pieces of silver."

As Paul preached the Gospel to these people, we see the result of their actions in verse 19 when the Scriptures said that they burned those things which caused them to do wrong. They didn't just talk about getting right with God, but they proved it by their actions.

As I travel and preach revival meetings on a weekly basis, one of the things I feel people lack is what we see in the verses above. Let me explain! I will preach a sermon that brings conviction upon someone's life. This results in them walking the aisle to confess that sin to God. Now what I have seen many times is these same people go home and do the exact same thing that they just supposedly got right with God about a few hours prior. The simple truth is, if you honestly get right with God, you will get rid of what caused you to do wrong. Repentance always brings action to do right.

Many people want to get right with God over certain things in their life. It may be a bad habit they have had for several years, it could be a one-time action which they performed, but whatever the case, they have the desire to do right. This is very commendable! But if we are going to overcome whatever it is that we desire to quit, we must do what these people did, completely get rid of what causes us to do wrong.

For instance, you will never overcome smoking by keeping a pack of cigarettes in your house. You will never overcome the wrong music by keeping that music in your house. You will never overcome any problem in your life by keeping whatever it is around just in case you want to go back to it. No, you must completely get rid of whatever it is that tempts you or causes you to do wrong. If it is a friend, stop running with that person. If it is a vice, get rid of that vice; don't keep it in your personal possessions. If it is an action, you must get rid of the cause of that action.

Always remember, if you keep something around, you will eventually feed that desire, which results in having to start all over again. Get rid of the cause of your sin, and you will have a much easier time overcoming the desire for that sin. Walking an aisle to get right with God is good, but getting rid of what causes the wrong to happen is even better. Repentance always brings actions to do right. So, prove your decision through your action to do right.